THIS BOOK IS DEDICATED TO:

Our canine pals, who remind us to feel pure joy every day

&

All the wonderful dogs awaiting their forever homes

TESTIMONIALS

The former German Shepherd Rescue president calls me his "favorite dog trainer":

"Julie was a staff trainer for Guide Dogs for the Blind. When I attended graduation there a few years back, I mentioned Julie's name, and the Guide Dogs folks lit up with smiles and said she was wonderful. Julie was also an adoption counselor for GSD rescue. Her dog, Fax, was a rescue and is now a therapy dog. Julie is the trainer I worked with when training Tyler. I would love to train with her again."

—Steve from California

This woman was feeling completely overwhelmed by her dog's excessive barking. It is a great example of how one personalized suggestion from me fixed a problem and made her feel good about being able to do it on her own:

"I just wanted to say THANK YOU for everything that I have learned from you! It's so empowering to pinpoint what I was doing wrong and change even the little things that make such a big difference."

—Nicki from Minnesota

This Portuguese water dog guardian was feeling frustrated with a problem behavior that had developed on walks:

"I started searching the Web after a failed attempt using an in-home dog-training service. Luckily, I found Julie and WebDogTrainer. In one chat Julie helped our dog go from re-fusing to go for a walk to happily walking with us. Julie's program and her articles have

made a tremendous difference in our dog's confidence and behavior. Julie's down-to-earth and humane advice can lead you to success if you are committed to helping your dog become a good citizen and contented companion."

—Sheryl from Colorado

The following attests to my calming, encouraging approach:

"Julie had an immediately calming effect on us as dog owners. She can explain the canine perspective and how we as humans can interact with our dog in a positive way. Julie was super patient with all of our questions."

—Sina and Ed from California

This man was already a well-read dog expert, but he needed a little personal assistance in how to gain more focus from his Great Dane during training:

"By following Julie's recommendations, my dog quickly curbed his bad behavior entirely."

—Frank from Washington

A senior woman was almost ready to give her Jack Russell up because she wasn't able to manage her high-energy dog:

"I really have to thank you for all the great help I got in order to train my Charles. He is like a new dog."

—Ann from South Carolina

IMAGINE LIFE
with a
WELL-BEHAVED DOG

IMAGINE LIFE

with a

WELL-BEHAVED DOG

★ A 3-Step Positive Dog-Training Program ★

Julie A. Bjelland

ST. MARTIN'S GRIFFIN

NEW YORK

www.stmartins.com

BOOK DESIGN BY AMANDA DEWEY

Library of Congress Cataloging-in-Publication Data

Bjelland, Julie A.
    Imagine life with a well-behaved dog : a 3-step positive
dog-training program / Julie A. Bjelland. —1st ed.
        p. cm.
    ISBN 978-0-312-59897-6
    1. Dogs—Training.   I. Title.
    SF431.B446 2010
    636.7'0887—dc22

                                                    2009033712

9   10   8

ACKNOWLEDGMENTS

I am very grateful to the people who helped this book come to be. I have a lot of people to thank along the way.

Special thanks to my remarkable editor, Michelle Richter at St. Martin's Press, for the care and attention you gave this book and for your kindness, helpful suggestions, and hard work. Thanks to my copy editor, Cynthia Merman, for being so helpful and thorough. Thanks to Elizabeth Catalano and Michelle McMillian and all of you who worked on the book at St. Martin's and brought your wonderful creativity to the project, and for all your hard work. Many thanks to my agents, Amberly Finnarelli and Andrea Hurst from Andrea Hurst Literary Management. Amberly, your fantastic attitude and warmth were so appreciated. Andrea, thanks for believing in me from the beginning. Your confidence in me helped make this happen and I will always be grateful.

Thanks to my boys, Oliver and Eliot, for all the joy you bring to my life and for inspiring me to write the book. Life is much fuller with you in it and the world much brighter. Out of all the boys in the world, I got the best ones. Saumil, thank you for taking on all the extra roles and responsibilities of life. You were a constant source of support keeping me strong and balanced. Thanks to my mom, for the many hours you spent reading and discussing my material, for being the biggest part of my support system, and for believing I can do whatever I set my mind to do.

Thanks to Gaurav and Abhilasha for your amazing creativity and many late nights working on the Web site. It was wonderful to brainstorm with you, Anthony and Jiwen, and share the experience with people whom I treasure so much as friends. Thanks to Jeff Lippincott who went above and beyond as my mentor from Score. Your time and wisdom were greatly appreciated. Thank you to Todd for sharing your amazing talents and skills with me as my mentor at Guide Dogs for the Blind. Thanks to all of you at GDB who shared your time, skills, and smiles. You are an amazing organization that I am proud to have been a part of. Thank you to Petfinder, Dogtime, and Baywoof for use of articles and/or forum Q & As that I wrote for them. Thanks to Isadora for the training photos and Ariella for your help on Facebook and MySpace.

Thank you to all my friends and family who offered their support throughout the process.

CONTENTS

CONCLUSION: LET'S SAVE DOGS' LIVES TOGETHER   *213*

LETTER FROM JULIE

*What lies behind us and what lies before us are tiny matters
compared to what lies within us.*
~ Oliver Wendell Holmes ~

Hello! I just want to say how wonderful I think it is that you are picking up this book and taking the time to learn more about dogs. It shows how much you care about dogs and learning how to communicate better with them in our human world.

I wanted to write a book that could help you understand your dog a little better without getting too complicated. I know how busy life is and how fast the world is moving, and sometimes you just want things a little easier. Maybe you'd like your dog to learn your human ways and not jump all over guests when they arrive in your home, excessively bark, chew up your favorite things, and leave unwanted surprises in the corner. Perhaps you just want to walk your dog without feeling like your arm is being pulled off when another dog passes by. Wouldn't it be nice to call your dog to you and know he'll come?

You can actually teach your dog to listen to you. All of these objectives are possible—and more. Having a well-behaved dog really isn't complicated, but it does take patience, practice, and consistency. I'm pretty sure when you see the results you'll find your effort worth it. There are small things you could be doing right now to achieve your goals. After I teach you what those things are, you'll be amazed how much better your dog listens to you.

I'll teach you what you *shouldn't* be doing and what you *should*. Thanks to technology, we can communicate about your dog if you need to, through my Web site, www.webDog Trainer.com. Think of me as a coach for you and your dog.

I'll also talk about ways you may be approaching things in your life. Why would a dog trainer want to talk about that? Because, interestingly enough, your thoughts and behaviors actually affect your dog. Focusing only on the dog is only half of the whole process of having a well-behaved dog. Getting to the roots of human behavior is the necessary first step toward having a harmonious life with your dog.

My Web site serves as a sort of life coach for clients who are working with their dogs; I can be called your "dog life coach." People find that communicating with me is more than just asking questions about their dogs. It also is a way to work toward achieving goals and finding balance in their life so that they can be fully focused, patient, and ready to train their dogs better. Because your dog is so in tune with you, it isn't surprising that your actions affect him and his behavior.

Lowering stress levels, along with communicating more clearly with your dog, could be a big part of your personal experience. Therefore, communication between clients and me might involve not only specific dog-related things, but also include managing frustration so you can be a better dog guardian.

I want to offer the same dog life coach benefits to readers of this book. I'm here for you if you need motivation or encouragement at any time. Maybe you want to talk about how frustrated you are and need a little friendly support. I'll provide it. Want to share how great your dog is, or have a special story to contribute? I'd love to hear about it. Need advice on a behavior issue? Just bark and I'll come running. I love connecting with you and offering support and guidance as you need it.

Connections make the human experience meaningful. I hope that being available when you need it will make you reach your goals and have a better life with your dog!

This book combines old-fashioned, small-town friendliness with supportive technology. Since talking with a dog trainer one-on-one can cost hundreds of dollars, I wanted to come up with a way for everyone to have really useful information about their dogs and even a way to ask a dog trainer about their own dog, without it costing too much. For a very reasonable cost, you'll get the information you need about your dog through the book *and* direct contact with me if you have any additional questions.

This is a unique, innovative, affordable way to teach *you* how to have a well-behaved dog and a better life. You don't have to be a professional dog trainer to teach your dog; you just need the information explained well so that you can learn how to teach your dog yourself. Having a coach to help you along the way will move you even higher on your path to attaining your goals.

Because I have a dog-training program on my Web site, I've had contact with people from all over the world. This has given me a special view of what most people want to know about dogs. I've learned about daily struggles with dogs, goals, and the mistakes most people make. So I created a book to answer those questions. I don't answer every single question you can ever think of, but I've covered the most common ones. And you can discuss any lingering questions with me through my site.

Some people will pick up this book and something will just click for them and it will go really well. Others may not be able to put the necessary consistency into their training program and thus won't reach their goals. We can't control everything, so your results won't always depend on my information but also on what you are *personally* putting into the program. But if you consistently follow my guidelines, you can have an off-leash dog who comes when you call, responds to your commands, and behaves the way you've asked him to.

Those of you with puppies, senior dogs, or dogs with special needs should consider adjustments in relation to health and exercise abilities as appropriate to your dog.

There are some extreme situations that cannot be fixed with this program, and you may want to seek an in-home trainer, but you'll be better educated and prepared if that happens. If this book keeps a few dogs that might have been given up in their forever homes, or helps you and your dog have a better, happier life, then I have reached my goal. If at any time you need personal advice about your own unique dog, or maybe just a little positive encouragement yourself, you can contact me at www.webDogTrainer.com.

Imagine life with *your* well-behaved dog.

Julie

IMAGINE LIFE

with a

WELL-BEHAVED DOG

ABOUT THE BOOK, ME, AND MY DOG

My Background

I grew up in Minnesota and had a childhood affinity with dogs on the farm and a natural ease with them. I discovered that I had a knack for teaching and for soothing animals. When I am training a dog, we become connected, and it shows. I can teach you how to have that connection.

As a vet tech, I became known for being good with the dogs who were difficult to handle because I had a way of calming them. My training as a vet tech and at Guide Dogs for the Blind, combined with my natural abilities with and love for dogs and all animals, helped me create my own dog-training business, which developed into the Web site.

My experience with GDB meant a lot because I was able to actually see what dogs can accomplish and how they help people, even saving lives.

One of the dogs I helped train saved someone's life. She was starting to cross an intersection when a car ran a red light. It would have hit her if her guide dog had not pulled her back to the curb, just as he had been trained to do. It was wonderful to hear how my training efforts helped. Guide Dogs for the Blind is an outstanding organization that offers guide dogs for the visually impaired at no cost.

Starting My Own Training Business

Over the years, I discovered a passion for obedience training and behavior modification and eventually started my own dog-training business. I enjoy the one-on-one contact with people and helping them learn how to communicate better with their dogs. It is very rewarding to help improve people's lives by teaching them how to have happy, successful relationships with their dog. I hear the word "Wow" a lot on our first sessions when they witness what their dog is capable of so quickly.

Before working with me, a lot of my clients had enrolled their dog in other training programs only to get their dog home and not know how to follow up with the training. It is common for a dog to listen only to the person who actually does the obedience with him, so once the trainer is gone, the dog doesn't listen to his guardian. While this method does train the dog, it can fail at home if the guardian doesn't learn—and use—the proper methods of reinforcing the training.

My training methods are unique, because I actually have most of the dog handling done by the guardians and not me. I teach them what to do. This creates a stronger bond between the dog and the guardian and the confidence to follow through when I'm not there. We also discuss dog behavior, dog body language, human psychology, and other tips that help them to understand their dogs better. The combination of learning technique and a little dog vs. human psychology are the winning components to having a well-behaved dog!

Many people contact me through my Web site because they sense they can trust me. They often tell me that they feel secure and competent in every aspect of their life *except* how to manage their dog's behavior, and they are embarrassed that they can't resolve it. They feel (correctly) that I won't judge them. I know that I learn better when someone explains something well to me and provides me with encouragement and motivation, so that is how I've learned to teach too.

webDogTrainer.com Is Born

Prior to writing this book I formed the webDogTrainer Web site; it has been very gratifying to see my methods help people from all over have success and the dog they always wanted. It has given me valuable information on what kinds of help people need with their dogs and made me realize how training through words can help a lot of people. People often just need a little support to get them through a difficult phase with their dog or quick tips to help resolve problem behaviors.

The Book

I've taken everything I've learned from my years as a dog trainer and from answering questions from people about their dogs to create this book. Offering the ability to ask me a personal question about your own dog and situation just makes this process even more successful. My hope is that this book becomes an important resource for teaching people how to have a great life with their dog and for keeping more dogs in their forever homes.

About My Dog

To the right is a photo of my sweet dog Fax, along with the two other big joys in my life, my sons, Eliot and Oliver. The funny thing is, dog training actually prepared me to be a good mother. Understanding how calm, clear, consistent expectations mixed with positive rewards turns out to be good for kids *and* dogs.

I adopted Fax through German Shepherd

Rescue and he turned from an unwanted problem dog into a happy, well-behaved pet who became a therapy dog and even helped me train other dogs. Rescuing dogs is my mission and Fax is a clear example of how good training can save a dog's life.

Overview

Does this sound familiar? Your dog jumps on everyone who enters your house; you dread another walk where your dog pulls you down the road. You stand in front of the dog-training section at the bookstore and feel overwhelmed. All you want is serenity at home, but these books are intimidating, filled with theories like operant and classical conditioning.

Wait! There's hope. *Imagine Life with a Well-Behaved Dog* is straightforward and encouraging, and you can actually contact me if you have questions. This is exactly what you need.

This combined book and innovative online training program can change the way you communicate with your dog. Because each dog's situation is unique, webDogTrainer.com complements the book so you can communicate directly with me about your own dog. Often, one personalized tip solves a behavior problem quickly. Therefore, offering the positive, one-on-one training program in print and then being able to connect personally with me results in a combination that can be particularly successful.

If you are thinking of adopting a new dog, this book includes tips on adopting an adult or puppy as well as where to adopt. Additionally, I can help you pick the right dog for your family.

Imagine Life with a Well-Behaved Dog contains all the information you need to make your dog happy, confident, secure, and able to understand and follow rules. It teaches you how to train your dog.

The program's success is the result of combining human psychology, dog psychology, and techniques in an uncomplicated way. You'll learn how to understand your dog's natural behavior, identify the effect of your own actions, establish personal training goals, and progress through beginning obedience to advanced off-leash training. Along the way, you will also learn how to fix or prevent common behavior problems.

Imagine Life with a Well-Behaved Dog is a user-friendly, motivating, practical guide for all people who are thinking of adopting a dog, already have a dog, or work with dogs and are not looking to win a title competition but just want to have a harmonious life with their dog. I hope to put you at ease, show the most efficient, successful way of training, and motivate you to succeed. The program is designed to help you understand your dog. I donate a portion of proceeds to charities that share my passion for helping dogs.

WebDogTrainer.com has given me extensive information on what people really require to succeed with their dog. The program is unique in helping people understand the stages of training. I've discovered most people have three main problems:

- They aren't communicating their needs properly to their dog.
- Their dog's specific energy needs are not being met.
- They are making small mistakes that have a big impact on the dog's behavior.

Certain sections focus on specific age ranges of dogs, particular limitations, or problem behaviors that are not applicable to all households.

The Online Personal Advice

Want to contact me? You can! I want to help you and your dog by offering my personal guidance, encouragement, and motivation to you individually, through my Web site. Use the promotional code IMAGINE at www.webDogTrainer.com, where you can easily log in and ask me questions. Whether you have a particular dog behavior issue or could use motivation, I am here for you if you need it.

I look forward to connecting with you on my site!

Your Dog Loves Who You Are

My goal in life is to be as good a person
as my dog already thinks I am.
~Anonymous~

Everyone has days where everything just seems to go wrong. Days filled with so much stress from work, deadlines, laundry, traffic, housecleaning, and errands that we feel like

we might melt under the pressure. Days where you do something for everyone else and don't have enough hours in the day.

Need someone to just love you for you? People with dogs have already discovered the secret. This beautiful creature will love you no matter what. Your dog doesn't care what kind of car you drive, how messy your house is, how much money you have, how smart or good-looking you are, or what you do for a living. All your dog sees is someone he loves and wants to make happy. Your dog thinks you are perfect, even if you aren't.

I asked a group of people who have dogs the following question: "What does your dog mean to you? How does he enhance your life?" Here are some of their responses:

Knowing you have someone who's waiting for you and will express with every bone in his cute little body how much he missed you! (Even if it was just a trip down to the mailbox!)

My dog brings hope and joy into my life, and a sense of purpose well beyond just going through the motions of life and making a living. From taking good care of her, I have started to take better care of myself. I have gotten more in touch with my spiritual side. It is no wonder that dogs are used so successfully in therapy.

She makes me smile, makes me feel better when I am down, makes me laugh, and sometimes just makes me get up out of bed when I don't want to. She is my soul mate and my best friend.

My senior has been through a lot of life changes and emotional times with me. She has always been there for me, knew when I was upset and would be close, lick my face, and cuddle. And she loves me no matter what. If I'm sick, she stays close but won't bother me. She definitely knows when I'm down or upset and tries her hardest to make it all better.

Walking in the door at the end of a long day at work and them being so happy to see me makes my life whole.

My dog is someone I can tell everything to and he won't blab. If I am in a bad mood he still loves me. Thinks I am a much bigger and better person than I am.

A considerate cuddling partner for nighttime TV watching.

Love your dog back by learning how to communicate with him so he can just love you without complications. A well-behaved dog gets to spend more time with you because he is more of a part of your life; he gets to live indoors with you, go on camping trips, to friend's houses, and to outdoor events. Dogs who are not trained well generally stay home alone more.

Make the decision to put in the effort. Take your dog for a walk and experience the joy of life through his eyes. Then come home and give him a body massage and recognize how much happiness your dog brings to your life.

After reading this book you'll have the skills needed to really understand your dog, meet his needs, communicate *your* needs, and truly experience the joy of sharing your life with this beautiful creature. Imagine life with a well-behaved dog.

The Wondrous Dog

Dogs have been trained to do all sorts of extraordinary things, which demands even more of our respect for this spectacular creature. They perform important services for humans and have saved many lives when trained in emergency response and during war. Dogs help police as special K9 officers, are the eyes for the blind, the ears for the deaf, and the assistant for the disabled.

Dogs in the military have been used for many important tasks, such as casualty search, detecting explosives, and assisting in patrols. K9 dogs help police departments in many duties, such as drug sniffing, catching criminals, and protection. Dogs risk their lives for us. Search-and-rescue dogs assist in rescue missions after natural disasters. Their incredible sense of smell has been responsible for saving many missing humans. Our world is safer with dogs in it.

Guide dogs are wondrous and extraordinary. My friend Aerial Gilbert (see photo below right), who works as outreach manager at Guide Dogs for the Blind, has this to say about her guide dog, Splash: "Having a guide dog is the closest thing to getting to walk like I did when I could see. Now if I get lost it is an adventure, with my best friend by my side. Splash is like a fine blend of a spouse, best girlfriend, and child all rolled into one."

Hearing dogs are trained to notify their human of sounds such as smoke detectors, doorbells, phones ringing, alarm clocks, oven timers, their name being called, and a crying child. Assistance dogs can perform all kinds of tasks for the disabled, such as turning lights on/off, picking up dropped items, standing as a brace for support, opening doors, retrieving the telephone and medications, and helping someone get dressed. They can even be taught to provide individual support that is unique to the disabled person's needs.

Additionally, because dogs have such a powerful sense of smell, they can detect leaks in underground gas pipes. Farmers sometimes use dogs to determine when their cows are in heat. They can track and find missing people. Research shows they can even be trained to detect cancer in humans. Seizure-alert dogs can be trained to detect when epileptics are about to have a seizure, even before the human knows. This can enable the person to get in a safe position for the seizure (not on stairs, for example). Some of these dogs are even trained to push a special emergency button. Well-trained dogs happily perform incredible tasks to help us.

The wondrous dog is an awe-inspiring creature who deserves admiration. Whether you are thinking about adopting a dog or already have one, this book will teach you how to meet his needs and offer him the best life possible. In return, he offers you never-ending, unconditional love.

1

ADOPTING A DOG

My sunshine doesn't come from the skies,
it come from the love in my dog's eyes.
~Anonymous~

Thinking of Adopting a Dog?

It is very emotional and exciting to fall in love with a dog and want to take him home, but there are a lot of factors to consider to determine what kind of dog is best for you. As a dog trainer, I've come across a lot of problem behavior in dogs because guardians weren't aware how essential it is to meet their dog's needs. Many dogs don't get all the exercise they need. If you meet your dog's needs, you will have a great companion full of love for you. If you don't meet his needs, you may run into problem behavior that can be a nightmare.

What Breed Is Right for You?

Just like people, dogs have individual personalities. Some dogs are highly energetic, others are calm and passive; some dogs are very social, and others not. If you have your heart set on a particular breed, you should search within that breed and find the dog that best matches your lifestyle. Also a mixed breed has the best of two or more breeds, plus is generally healthier and less prone to genetic problems.

Examine Your Personality

Before you even consider what breed of dog, examine your life a little to discover what kind of dog would best "match" you. If you love the outdoors and are very athletic, planning to do a lot of running, hiking, or dog sports, consider a medium to large size, high-energy dog who can keep up with you. If you like to stay home and don't really like to walk very much, you may want a mellower dog as a companion, such as a senior dog. Dogs are like people—they all differ in personality and needs. Are you high energy and always on the go, or are you laid back? Are you affectionate, looking for a dog to cuddle, and would be disappointed in a dog who is more aloof? Understanding your personality and matching it to a dog's personality is crucial.

Consider Your Lifestyle

Are you too busy for a dog? Do you have enough time to spend with your dog every day? How much space do you have in your home? If you live in a tiny apartment, you might not have space for a large breed dog. Do you have a backyard or do you live in a high-rise apartment? Do you have another pet in the home? Can they all get along harmoniously? Do you often entertain formally at your home? Consider these factors before you decide what kind of dog to adopt. Study the different breeds to learn more about what may suit your lifestyle the best.

Are You Assertive or Passive?

Assertive people are direct and natural leaders. They can be commanding and can give orders easily. Passive people are more comfortable being a follower than a leader. They are often more patient and approach things more carefully. Strong-willed or dominant dogs may be difficult for a naturally passive person to handle. Dominant dogs require strong leadership or they may rule the house.

How Old Are the Members of Your Family?

If you have children under 8, you probably shouldn't get a puppy under 6 months of age because puppies have sharp teeth and claws that can hurt sensitive skin. You also ought not to get a toy-size dog because they can be very fragile and get hurt easily. With small children, you're be better off getting an adult dog that is larger than a toy dog. It is important that it has a "known good history" with children. Dogs over age 2 or 3 can be ideal because they have already gone through the difficult puppy and adolescence stages.

Do not expect children to take over all the dog care, no matter how much they promise they will (remember their promises to put dirty clothes in the hamper, return the milk carton to the fridge . . .). They may be able to assist you, but as the parent, *you* will have the responsibility. Assess your energy level and your amount of free time. It is a lot of work keeping up with children, and a dog adds one more big responsibility. Supervise your young children around the dog at all times. (Children can be unpredictable and do things like pull tails or whiskers and cause the dog to feel threatened.) Don't leave your children with the dog unattended, and you will have to teach them about being gentle and what areas are off-limits to touch. Also consider your children's friends who will visit—you will have to supervise them around the dog too.

If there are elderly or physically challenged people in the household, a large or young or energetic dog could knock them over and cause injury.

Dogs live 10 to 15 years or more. Adopting a dog is a long-term commitment that you should take very seriously. The reason there are so many homeless dogs is that the guardian and the dog were mismatched, not because there is something wrong with the dog. First-time guardians often do not realize how much effort is required to have a happy, healthy, well-behaved dog. Millions of dogs are killed in shelters every year, so carefully consider this very big decision before bringing a dog into your home.

Can You Afford a Dog?

Here is a breakdown of estimated cost, taken from the ASPCA, for the first year, in addition to the adoption fees. (Small breeds weigh less than 20 pounds as adults, medium breeds weigh 21–50 pounds, large breeds weigh 51+ pounds.)

First-Year Costs of Owning a Dog			
Costs	Small Dog	Medium Dog	Large Dog
Annual Costs			
Food[1]	$55	$120	$235
Recurring medical[2]	$210	$235	$260
Toys/treats	$40	$55	$75
License	$15	$15	$15
Health insurance (optional)[3]	$225	$225	$225
Misc.	$35	$45	$65
Annual Total	**$580**	**$695**	**$875**
Capital Costs			
Spay/neuter	$190	$200	$220
Other initial medical[4]	$70	$70	$70
Collar/leash	$25	$30	$35
Carrier bag	$40	$60	
Crate	$35	$95	$125
Training class	$110	$110	$110
Capital Total	**$470**	**$565**	**$560**
Special Costs			
Long-hair groom	$265	$320	$410
FIRST YEAR TOTAL	**$1,315**	**$1,580**	**$1,845**

1. Premium brand dry kibble
2. Exam, vaccinations, heartworm preventative, topical flea/tick preventative
3. Insurance coverage varies: some policies cover spay/neuter, vaccinations, and heartworm medication
4. Deworming, basic blood tests, microchip

Responsibilities of Having a Dog

I don't shed that much.
Just enough to decorate your brand-new dress pants.
~Steve D. Marsh, Dog-Ku~

What Does Your Dog Need?

It is important to know what actually goes into having a dog and taking care of him. It is easy to understand the benefits of having a dog and what he will bring to your life—a dog is a never-ending source of love without judgment. But in order to have a good life with your dog, you need to know what you are getting into and what your responsibility is. There would be a lot fewer dogs in shelters if everyone were fully prepared and aware of what it takes to raise a dog successfully.

YOUR JOB

1. Spay or neuter. This is extremely important.
2. License and register your dog. (There is a steep fine for unlicensed dogs.) The fees pay for things your dog would be proud of: animal control officers, state humane agents, animal cruelty investigators, care for strays, and return of lost dogs to their owners. Millions of dogs end up in shelters as lost or stray and only about 16 percent are reunited with their guardians, according to No Voice Unheard, a nonprofit animal advocacy organization. Make sure your dog always has an ID tag on with his name, your name, and your address and telephone number. A microchip is also a good idea—collars and tags can get separated from your dog. The chips can be "read" by most animal shelters and veterinary clinics.
3. Walk your dog twice a day for at least 30–45 minutes each. High-energy dogs need more, and senior dogs, puppies, and toy breeds need less. If you work all day, get up about an hour earlier to take the walk, feed your dog, and play a little. Repeat when you return home.
4. Give your dog lots of time with you and the family every day.
5. Feed your dog twice a day. Always fill their water bowl with new water daily.

6. Dog training. Dogs that are well trained are happier and more bonded with their guardians. They also get to spend more time with you because they are well behaved.
7. Clean up your dog's poop, in your yard and everywhere else.
8. Adult dogs have to have a veterinary exam at least annually and be current on all their vaccinations. Puppies require several more trips to the veterinarian the first year for additional vaccinations as well as spaying/neutering. Ask your veterinarian about cost, etc.
9. Brush, bathe, groom, cut nails, clean ears.
10. Flea/tick care and heartworm medication.
11. Oral care for your dog. Veterinarians recommend teeth brushing at home twice a week and annual professional cleanings.
12. Puppies require a tremendous amount of time and money their first year. You also have to housetrain them, which requires a lot more time on your part than it would for an adult dog.
13. You need a well-maintained fence at least 6 feet tall for a dog able to jump high, if you plan to have him off-leash in the backyard at all.
14. Dog hair has a way of attaching itself to *everything* and will require more cleaning on your part.
15. Arrange for care of your dog while you are away.
16. Extra expense. There is a lot of expense in having a dog, including veterinarian costs, food, supplies (leash, collar, ID tags, bedding), toys, chew bones, flea care, bathing, grooming, medical if he becomes ill, etc.

The Proper Way to Greet New Dogs

If you are new to the dog world, here are tips to help you and your family learn to greet dogs properly. Most dogs are friendly and will not bite, but they require respect. Never allow your child to run up to pet an unknown dog. You do not know that dog's history with children. Children can get bitten for many reasons, such as the fact that their fast movements can trigger a chasing prey response. The pitch of a child's voice is higher than an adult's and can sometimes startle a dog. Children are also shorter and closer to the dog's eye level, and the eye-to-eye contact can make a dog feel threatened. It is important to supervise young children to be sure they don't do things that make the dog uncomfortable, such as pulling his tail or ears or teasing him.

It can help to understand good dog-greeting etiquette. In a good greeting, two dogs come to each other in an arc, not a straight line, looking at each other, looking away, and then moving to smell each other. They do not approach each other directly face-to-face, and they do not make strong eye contact on the approach. The approach is calm, quiet, without direct eye contact, and using smell. Dogs use their sense of smell to get to know you too.

DOS AND DON'TS WHEN GREETING A DOG

- *Do* always ask the dog handler's permission to pet the dog. If your child is involved, go a step farther and ask if the dog is comfortable around children.
- *Do* offer your hand, palm down, for the dog to smell, and allow the dog to approach you. *Don't* approach the dog first. If the dog does not want to greet you, leave it at that and do not approach.
- *Don't* stare at the dog; instead, smile at the dog and then look away. When you take your eyes off the dog you are signaling that you are not a threat.
- *Don't* bend over the dog.
- *Don't* pet the dog on top of the head; it is better to pet on the chest or back.
- *Don't* approach the dog from behind.
- *Don't* scream or make fast movements; stay calm and quiet.
- *Don't* kiss the dog or put your face near the dog's face.
- *Don't* greet a new dog who is sleeping or eating.
- *Do* observe the dog's body language and *don't* pet a dog showing signs of being uncomfortable, fearful, or aggressive. Signs a dog may be uncomfortable: He hides behind something or someone, he tries to avoid an interaction, his tail is tucked between his legs, he is looking away, he is shaking, or he growls.

When you understand how to greet new dogs you will feel more comfortable and the experience will be positive.

Adopting a Puppy

Puppies are a lot of fun and their cuteness can touch you deep inside your heart. It is hard to resist adorable puppies. But they are also a lot of work! If you are thinking of adopting a puppy, you should know what to expect. Many people bring home a cute puppy only to find that it chews up everything, poops inside the house, and keeps them up at night. That puppy gets bigger, more difficult to handle, and ends up homeless at the shelter.

A new puppy is a bit like a new baby. Expect to get up every 2 to 3 hours at night to bring him out to eliminate. Completely puppy-proof your home. You cannot leave puppies unattended in a room with wires, anything sharp, shoes, socks, poisonous plants, or a remote control. Puppies chew *everything*. The only way to stop this is to prevent it. You must observe your puppy at all times. When you can't, put him in a place that doesn't have anything you don't want chewed. You'll be responsible for a very important part of a puppy's life—socialization. How you bring up your puppy now can affect what kind of an adult he becomes.

You cannot expect your children to be responsible for your puppy's needs no matter how much they promise they will. Most children cannot be fully responsible for a dog until they become mature teenagers. The responsibility falls on you.

Do not adopt a puppy unless you are well informed of what it takes to raise a puppy, have done your homework, and understand his needs. A dog is a big 10- to 15-year responsibility and having a well-behaved dog takes a real commitment on your part.

As a dog trainer, I've seen many unprepared people adopt puppies. It is a sad situation to take a puppy from his mother and littermates and not give him a home he deserves. Many end up being relinquished at shelters after their guardians discover how much work it takes to raise a puppy. If you are going to adopt a puppy, plan ahead so that you know what to expect and how to do everything right to have a good relationship with your puppy throughout his life.

What is the earliest age you can adopt a puppy? Most breeders try to adopt out puppies between 7 and 10 weeks of age. Do not adopt a puppy that is younger than this. Taking puppies away from their mothers and littermates at such an early age can affect their ability to relate to other dogs, as well as skip important lessons learned from their family.

Adopting an Adult Dog

Many adult and senior dogs find themselves in shelters because their guardians died, entered a nursing home, or moved someplace that didn't allow dogs. One day they are happily snoozing on the sofa, the next day they are alone in a cage, through no fault of their own. All they want is a new family to love and to love them.

BENEFITS OF ADOPTING AN ADULT DOG

- What you see is what you get. Unlike puppies, you know how big your dog ended up.
- You can match his personality to your lifestyle. It can be hard to predict what kind of dog a puppy will grow up to be.
- Adult dogs are generally house broken. According to the ASPCA, puppies need to be brought out to eliminate every hour, as well as after eating, playing, and naps.
- Puppies do not do well alone for long periods of time like an adult dog can.
- An adult dog has passed the "chew everything" phase.
- You'll sleep better at night with an adult dog. Puppies are very demanding at night!
- Puppies need a lot of trips to the veterinarian for vaccinations, neutering/spaying, etc. Your adult dog should be all set up.
- You can go out right away with an adult dog, exploring the world together. With a puppy you may have to wait until he is all up to date on shots, etc.

Adopting a Senior Dog

Adopting a senior dog has a lot of wonderful benefits. According to the Senior Dogs Project, many great older dogs are available for adoption and are often overlooked because of

their age. But these older dogs offer an extremely high-quality choice as companions for many reasons. Older dogs

- usually have had some obedience training.
- are generally housetrained.
- offer the best choice for families with young children, human seniors, and physically challenged individuals because they are generally calmer and better behaved.

- understand what "no" means.
- know what not to chew.
- are generally socialized to get along with humans, usually other dogs, and often even cats.
- are calmer.
- appreciate love and attention.
- let you do tasks at home.

Senior dogs are often the first ones killed in the shelter, simply because of their age. But they deserve so much more. Rescuing and fostering senior dogs are wonderful ways to "give back."

- can sit quietly next to you while you fold the laundry or read and actually let you finish.
- don't require as much intensive exercise as younger dogs.
- let you get a full night of sleep!

Adopting a Rescue/Shelter Dog

Many of the beautiful dogs featured in this book are rescue or shelter dogs. They are examples of the wonderful mixed-breed and purebred dogs found in rescue groups and shelters. There are so many great reasons to adopt a rescue/shelter dog. Millions of dogs are killed every year in shelters simply because there are not enough homes for them. Most of these dogs were given up because there was a mismatch in personality with the previous guardian, or people did not fully comprehend the responsibility of having a dog, not because there is something wrong with the dog.

Shelters offer a wide variety of dogs. You can find mixed breeds, pure breeds, and even puppies. According to the Humane Society of the United States, shelters carry 25–30 percent purebred dogs. If you want to adopt a particular breed, there are also many rescue organizations that specialize in certain breeds.

Good shelters and rescue organizations want to make the best matches possible and will work with you to find your ideal match. They have spent time

with the dogs and have gotten to know their needs and what kind of guardian would best match those needs. What a great way to find a dog that will fit in with your lifestyle! They often have adoption counselors who can help you find the right dog for you.

They are also receiving new dogs every day, so if you don't find what you are looking for on your first trip, don't be discouraged. You can be put on a waiting list for the kind of dog that may match you best.

Shelter/rescue dogs are a lot less expensive than dogs from a breeder, plus the cost should include spaying/neutering, shots, deworming, vaccinations, etc.

Visit a shelter on a day when you are not rushed. You need to spend some time with the dogs. If possible, bring along family members, since you are choosing a dog for everyone. Keep in mind that these dogs are under stress; it isn't natural to be locked up for weeks or longer. Be prepared for lots of frantic jumping and barking.

In preparation, I suggest that you read the section "Bringing Your Dog Home" (page 29) so you are prepared if you end up finding the dog of your dreams today. In addition, consider the questions below. Prior self-analysis should help you make a better choice.

Ask yourself

- Are you passive or assertive? Match that to the dog's personality. If you are dominant, you may not want a shy, submissive dog. If you are passive, you may not want a dominant dog.

- What is your energy level? Do you have the energy necessary to exercise an active dog every day? Do you want a jogging partner, or a dog who doesn't need as much exercise?
- Do you want a dog that is affectionate and wants to cuddle, or are you okay with a dog who doesn't need so much affection?
- How much time will the dog be left alone daily? Do you travel a lot? (Consider a dog walker or sitter if you get a high-energy, high-needs dog and plan to leave him alone a lot.)
- Are there other pets at home? Does your cat get along with dogs? Is your current dog good with other dogs?
- Are there small children or physically challenged individuals in your family who will have to be supervised with the dog? A young, energetic, large dog can jump on people, causing harm. (At the shelter, ask if a dog you like has a good "known" history with children.)
- Have you set aside a few days to a week to spend at home with your new dog until he gets used to his new life?
- Are you ready to bring the dog home today? Do you have all the supplies necessary? See "Bringing Your Dog Home," page 29.
- Why do you want to adopt a dog? Sometimes putting things down on paper helps evaluate things more clearly.

List your answers, plus anything else that is important to you:

_____

_____

_____

_____

_____

_____

_____

_____

_____

This list can help you stay focused on what would be right for you. It is a good idea to talk with the people who work at the shelter before going inside, as they may be able to introduce you to dogs who could meet your needs. It is an overwhelming experience to walk through the kennel area, but if you are prepared it can help.

If there is a dog you are interested in, ask if you can take him out of the kennel area to a patio or, even better, for a walk. That will give you a chance to spend one-on-one time with the dog away from the chaos of the other dogs. Observe the dog closely. Is he friendly, good with being handled? Examine your instincts as well. Ask about the dog's background and what is known about his history. Is the staff aware of any specific behavior problems? Is the dog neutered/spayed, fully vaccinated? If not, can that be done before you take him home?

If you find a dog you might want to adopt, take a few minutes to think about it. Go outside and discuss it with family members without the distraction of the dog. This is a big commitment. *Don't* rush into it. Were all your questions about the dog answered? If not, go back inside and ask more questions. Then go outside to think about it some more.

Think carefully about whether this dog will fit your lifestyle. Don't be impulsive and get a dog because you feel sorry for him. Evaluate your gut instincts. Get this dog only if you are absolutely 100 percent positive you want him, and want him now. If you are 99.9 percent sure, go home and think about it overnight.

Dog rescue groups often have adoption days where fosterers bring the dogs available for adoption and you can meet them in person. These dogs have often been living in the home of the person who is temporarily fostering them, so they generally have a great idea of what the dog is like.

Many rescue groups post information about each dog on their Web sites so you can have a good idea of who you would like to meet at adoption day. Also, if there is a dog you are particularly interested in on the Web site, I suggest contacting the group and asking about him. Sometimes fosterers are more likely to attend the adoption event if they know someone is interested in their dog. Or you can sometimes arrange special meetings between you and the fosterer.

It is easy to lose your focus with a cute dog in need of a home in front of you (or on your lap), so stay focused on what is right for you and your family. If you make the right decision now, you have the potential to have a wonderful life with your new companion. A good dog is a tired, well-trained dog, so plan lots of exercise and training for your new dog!

To locate your local animal shelter, check the Internet or the Yellow Pages under "animal shelter," "animal control," or "humane society." Volunteers who have a lot of knowledge and love of a particular breed usually run breed rescues. They've rescued these dogs and keep them in volunteer foster homes until suitable adopters are found. To locate a particular breed rescue, you can contact your local shelter or search online under the specific breed followed by the word "rescue" (e.g., basset hound rescue). Additionally, some rescue groups have all types of breeds rather than just one. Other good rescue dog online resources are petfinder.com, pets911.com, and adoptapet.com.

Check out Pet Guardian Angels of America (pgaa.com). I asked Ron, who started the site, to tell me a little more about it:

Pet Guardian Angels of America started "live" in July of 1998 with the goal of providing pet-related information to help our visitors better understand what kind of pet would fit their lifestyle and, once they owned a pet, to make sure the pet was well taken care of—emotionally and physically.

Today we provide that same information through informative links, book recommendations, and health and general articles. The site includes dog and cat breed selection guides, breed profiles, small mammal guides, domestic bird guides, and fish, reptile, and amphibian articles.

PGAA also maintains an actively growing rescue index by state with an Internet service that provides free adoption and surrender assistance to our visitors. Averaging 60-90 e-mails a month, we have been very successful in helping people find pets and pets find people. Please visit our Guest Opinion page to read some of the comments about this service.

PGAA welcomes all pet lovers to visit our site and to e-mail us if they need help in finding a pet, or in surrendering a pet when all other avenues have been exhausted.

Foster a Dog

If you find it in your heart to care for somebody else,
you will have succeeded.
~Maya Angelou~

Ruthie was found alone, trying to survive on a country road. She has a deformed hind leg, but it doesn't slow her down. She is a great example of how someone opened her arms to foster a dog in need. Here is a little something her foster mom had to say about Ruthie. "Ruthie is a true delight! She is as sweet as she is smart. Some people might think that Ruthie has a disability. However, as far as she is concerned, her only disability was the people who brought her into this world and then abandoned her. She will make a wonderful addition to a 'special' family." Ruthie is a success story because she found her loving forever home thanks to all the people who got involved to help her.

Many rescue groups are run by volunteers and have lots of dogs in need of foster care while they are waiting for adoption. These wonderful people often visit shelters and save great dogs who would otherwise be killed due to lack of space. They try to get them adopted, but in the meantime are often desperate for help to foster them temporarily. It is a fantastic way to give back to help dogs, plus it can give you a chance to get to know what kind of dog might suit your lifestyle best. Fostering a dog can be challenging but also extremely rewarding, and you will be making a life-or-death difference for the dog you foster. If there is a particular breed you would like to foster, you can contact your local rescue group for that breed. If you are open to breed, contact your local humane society or shelter for more information.

The Worst Place to Adopt a Dog

Buying a puppy from a pet store or discount puppy breeder/puppy mill tops the list of worst places to adopt a dog. If you buy your dog from a pet store or online from a "discount" breeder, there is a very real chance he came from a puppy mill. Some stores do adoption days for dogs coming from a shelter; shelter dogs are okay to adopt because the shelter doesn't support puppy mills.

What is a puppy mill exactly? After watching a report by Lisa Ling on *Oprah* that took a hidden camera into puppy mills, I was horrified and shocked. I knew they were bad, but I did not know just how bad.

Let's take a tour of a puppy mill together. Hundreds of dogs are kept in small wire cages with wire flooring. The dogs are dirty, covered in urine and feces, with large patches of their fur missing and skin covered with sores. Several dogs are kept in each small cage, and the adult dogs often do not even know how to walk because they never have been out of the cage! They can spend ten years or more in these tiny cages together with no medical care. The females are forced to breed every cycle, producing hundreds of puppies each. The females are covered in tumors from overbreeding. When the dog can no longer reproduce, she is shot. Some of the dogs have had a long tube hammered down their throat to damage their vocal chords so they cannot bark. The dogs are not socialized and have never had a human pet them. Many have chains on their necks that are so tight their bloody skin has grown through the chain.

Once these breeding dogs have their puppies, the puppy mill owners take the puppies, clean them, fluff them up to make them look cute, and sell them in bulk to pet stores or online as discount breeders. If you knew this cute puppy's mother was suffering for years in a cage to produce this puppy, would you want to finance this operation, or would you want to do what you could to shut it down? If you buy a puppy that originates from this kind of place, you are paying for it to continue. These puppy mill dogs are cute on the outside, but they are overbred, which can cause major behavioral and physical (genetic) problems that can end up costing you a lot of money and suffering down the road.

How can you know if a dog came from a puppy mill or a reputable breeder? Buy a puppy from a breeder only if you can actually visit the location and see the condition of the mother and other dogs. If you buy from a breeder online and have the puppy shipped to you, so you cannot physically visit the area, you don't know if it comes from a puppy mill. You get what you pay for; do not be fooled by a discount breeder.

The Difference Between a Dog from a Puppy Mill and a Dog from a Reputable Breeder

A dog's genes and temperament play an important role in how he turns out. Genes affect a dog's health and his temperament, and the way the dog is raised in his first few weeks also affects his later behavior. If a parent has health problems, they will likely be passed down to the puppies. Responsible breeders do not breed a dog who has known health problems. Additionally, if the puppy is not properly socialized or exposed to his surroundings and people, he could become aggressive or withdrawn or otherwise not the best friend you envisioned.

Pick a breeder who appropriately socializes the puppy during the first 8 weeks and breeds only healthy dogs. Puppy mills do not have guidelines and are interested only in breeding the most dogs to make the most money. A breeder at a puppy mill is not going to be honest with you, so the only way to truly know if the breeder is reputable is to visit in person. Be careful of magazine and newspaper ads advertising discount puppies; they most likely come from a puppy mill. Do not be tempted to save money here or you may pay dearly in the long run with health and behavior problems.

If you are set on buying a puppy, contact the American Kennel Club (akc.org) to help you find a reputable breeder. Members of this organization are supposed to follow strict regulations for breeding and raising puppies, but there may be some breeders who slip through the cracks and don't follow the rules. Do your own research and visit the breeder and ask to see the mother. A reputable breeder will be glad to show you. Ask questions. How old is the mother? How many litters has she had? Where do the dogs live? Are the puppies in kennels or with the family? Go look. The father may not be available to see because good breeders do not generally use the same father every time.

Listen to your gut. I've always relied on my intuition to tell me if something feels right or not. Do not get caught up in how cute the puppy is and buy him without knowing where he came from. If you feel sorry for it and buy it, you are supporting an industry that is extremely cruel to dogs. You will pay more for a puppy from reputable breeders, and you should. These dog lovers put time and money into raising healthy puppies. The long-term investment in the dog will be worth it.

Why are we producing all these dogs in horrible conditions when we have perfectly good dogs needing homes in our shelters? Shelter dogs and rescue dogs make wonderful companions and, with a little training, you can have the dog you always wanted and feel great that you adopted a dog in need rather than supported grossly inhumane puppy mills.

What Can One Person Do?

Adopt your dog from a shelter or rescue group and never buy from a puppy store or unknown breeder. Get your dog spayed or neutered to prevent the overpopulation of dogs. Spread the word about puppy mills. Learn more, educate others, volunteer at a shelter or rescue group. Dogs love us and depend on us (and vice versa), let's work together. Adopt from your local shelter or rescue organization!

Giving a Dog as a Gift

Here's a fun and more responsible alternative to giving a dog as a gift. As you have learned, adopting a dog requires a lot of forethought and responsibility to pick the right "match" so instead of buying a dog for someone as their gift, you can try this more responsible alternative: If you know someone who really wants to get a dog, give him or her this book and a promise to help them pick out the right dog for their needs. You can even make up a cute, handmade certificate that states your promise to help them pick out the dog, wrapped up with this book inside of a dog bowl or with a box of dog treats. This way, you are a part of giving them the dog but also responsible enough to help them pick the dog that would be their best match.

2

PREPARING FOR A NEW DOG

Anybody who doesn't know what soap tastes like
never washed a dog.
~Franklin P. Jones~

Bringing Your Dog Home

Adopting a dog is exciting! Here are tips that will help make the transition of bringing home your new dog easier so that you can start your life together successfully.

Rules for a Successful Adoption

1. **Dogproof inside and outside your home.** Put away or out of reach anything that may be hazardous, like cleaners; chemicals; pesticides; rodent, insect, or snail bait; electrical cords, etc. Also consider plants that could be poisonous both indoors and out. Visit ASPCA Animal Poison Control Center at apcc .aspca.org and type "toxic plants for dogs" in the search box for a listing on-line, or call their 24-hour toll-free number, 888-426-4435. Or ask your veterinarian for a complete list.

2. **Have your supplies ready.** You need a leash, collar, food, bowls for food and water, toys, bones for chewing, grooming tools. Also think about getting an appropriate crate and a baby gate to close off certain areas in your home. Special cleaning supplies may also be needed that neutralize urine odor if you will be working on housetraining, along with a pooper-scooper and bags.

3. **Before you bring your dog home, the very first thing you should do is take him for a really long walk** (about an hour or more for medium- and larger-size dogs who are younger than age 5 or so; small/toy dogs and senior dogs need less). The idea here is to drain your dog's pent-up energy and nervousness. This also gives you both a chance to bond. Your goal from now on is to make sure to exercise your dog at least twice a day until he is tired out (meaning he lies down to rest after the exercise).

4. **Introduce the home in a calm, relaxing way.** Keep your dog on-leash initially and allow him to explore some areas of your home. Show him the area outside where he is allowed to eliminate right away.

5. **Stay home with your dog for the first few days to a week, if possible.** A little extra effort early on makes a big difference! Taking time off work now will pay off in the future because you were able to establish all the rules early on before your dog acquired habits you would have to work to break.

6. **Be patient during the adjustment period.** Some dogs settle in immediately, but others may take 2 to 3 weeks or even longer to adapt to their new home. Dogs who have been housetrained may even revert back to having accidents during this adjustment period. Be patient; offer your calm, clear, confident leadership during this time. Your dog may have been through a lot, and it can

take time for him to trust that this is his home from now on. Establish a routine early on, including regular exercise, which will help him feel more secure.

7. **Make a trip to the veterinarian.** Make sure your dog is healthy and up-to-date on his vaccinations. Also, get your dog spayed or neutered right away, if necessary. You don't want to contribute to more unwanted pets!

8. **Get an identification tag and rabies and license tags.** You can get an ID tag with your dog's name and contact information at any pet store. Check with your veterinarian to get your rabies tag. To find out where to license your dog, do an Internet search for "dog license [your city and state]."

9. **Keep your dog on-leash for the first two weeks** so that you can teach him what is good behavior and what is not acceptable. This may sound extreme, but it is one of the fastest ways to teach proper behavior in the home and I have seen a high success rate with this method. When your dog is on-leash near you, your timing will be very good to stop bad behaviors and reward good ones. The time you put into this early will be well worth the reward later. Attach the leash to yourself and have your dog be with you and go where you go in the house. If you need to leave the home before your dog is housetrained and trustworthy, you'll need to either crate train him (see "Crate Training," p. 37 or keep him in a closed-off, safe space. See the housetraining section (p. 44) for more information.

10. **As a family, create rules and goals you expect from your dog,** ideally before bringing him home, but especially before allowing him off-leash in the home. It is a good idea to have a family meeting and discuss and agree on your expectations of the dog. Will he be allowed on the couch, the bed, and all rooms of the house? Where will he sleep and eat? Who will walk the dog and clean up after him? As a family you must all be consistent with your decisions or you will confuse your dog and he probably will not follow your rules.

11. **Start training.** Having a well-trained dog is a wonderful experience. Dogs who are trained well are happier and get to go out with you more and are a joy to have around.

12. **Enjoy your dog!** With the proper care and training, your life will be filled with joy with this new addition to your family!

Bonding with Your Dog

A dog is the only thing on earth that loves you more
than he loves himself.
~Josh Billings~

Bonding with your dog is an important process in having a successful relationship with your new canine pal. Spending time with your dog helps create that bond. Playtime, close physical contact (being indoors with you), training, and living by clear rules in the household are all a part of that bond. Dogs who are closely bonded with their human do better in training because they value and trust their human more than dogs who are not as bonded. If your house rules are clear and you have consistent expectations of your dog, he will feel more secure and trust you, leading to a greater bond.

Think about allowing your dog to sleep in your room at night, especially if you are gone a lot during the day. It is better not to share your bed, but both of you can have your own bed in the same room. If your dog won't stay on his bed, he may prefer sleeping in a dog crate in your room. Time together sleeping, listening to your breathing, can bond you.

Dogs like to spend time with other dogs, but they need a lot of time with their human. Imagine you are out on a walk, and your dog sees other dogs in the distance. If your dog is bonded to you, and has had a healthy mix of time with you and time with other dogs, then it will be easy for you to maintain control over your dog. But if your dog has not bonded to you, it is much harder to regain his focus onto you. Likewise, if he is never around other dogs, he will be harder to control. A good mix of solid bonding time with you as well as occasional time with other dogs is ideal.

It is important not to allow your dog to greet every passing dog, because you set him up not to be able to walk past other dogs. You decide whom he greets and when. Don't let your dog pull you toward another dog just because he wants to; it is your decision as the leader whether or not to approach. (See "Being a Calm, Clear, Consistent Leader," p. 71.) Your dog should be able to pass by other dogs, and if you choose to, he can greet another dog.

Therefore, bonding is more than just a way to love your dog; it is also the first step in having a well-behaved dog. Once you and your dog have established a trusting, highly valued bond, the rewards will be great.

Feeding Schedule

Feed your dog at least twice a day (feed puppies under 5 months 3–4 times a day), and have fresh water in his bowl at all times. It is important that your dog is able to go outside to pee and poop about 15 minutes after eating. After a dog eats, his bowels are stimulated. If you are working away from home, a good schedule is to walk your dog immediately when you get up in the morning. When you return from the walk, let him rest for up to an hour, if possible, before feeding, while you get ready, have breakfast, etc. Then feed your dog and take him outdoors before you leave for work. When you return from work, exercise him, then feed him an hour later and again take him out to eliminate within 15 minutes. Leave the food bowl down for about 15 minutes, then pick it up and put it away. Check with your veterinarian to determine the proper amount of food.

Watch your dog's weight. With more exercise he needs more food and with less exercise he needs less food. Adjust the food according to how his weight looks to you. It is important to keep your dog at an optimal weight for health reasons. Check with your veterinarian on what weight is best for your dog.

The serious condition bloat occurs when your dog's stomach overfills with food, water, or air. The enlarged stomach can actually rise and twist, and once the rotation occurs the blood supply can be cut off and the dog can die.

To prevent bloat, feed your dog 2 to 3 times a day rather than one large meal. It's very important not to exercise your dog immediately before or after eating. Avoid vigorous exercise, excitement, and stress one hour before and after meals.

There are several symptoms to look out for—your dog unsuccessfully attempts to vomit, isn't acting like himself, or has a tight, bloated abdomen. It is more common in larger, deep-chested dogs over age 2. If your dog falls into this category, be aware of the warning signs and preventive measures and ask your veterinarian for more information.

Dog Food

Today's dog food choices can be overwhelming. I suggest that you first talk with your veterinarian about your dog to determine if there are any health conditions that might influence which type of dog food to buy. There are many foods available created for dogs with special needs, such as senior dogs, active dogs, puppies, and dogs with dietary restrictions. Your dog's skin and coat condition can also be a factor as to what type of dog food you choose or what supplements you may wish to add to his diet.

If you make your own dog food, consider adding supplements made for dogs, such as vitamins, minerals, amino acids, etc., to help complete the nutritional balance. Some people choose to feed their dogs vegetarian diets, where the dog receives his protein from plant sources instead of meat sources. This alternative can work for your dog as long as you include the right ratio of protein, grain, and vegetables. There are vegetarian and even vegan premade dog foods available. Your veterinarian can suggest what supplements as well as what ratio of protein, grains, and vegetables to use.

As a lover of all animals and a vegetarian, I feel it is worth saying that if you are going to feed your dog standard dog food with meat as the source of protein, think about buying organic dog foods. Organic meats are more eco-friendly, there are higher standards for how humanely these animals are treated, and they are healthier because they do not contain hormones and chemicals. You can also look online for a list of cruelty-free brands of dog food.

Dietary changes must be done slowly to prevent digestive upset. If you switch the type of dog food, do it over the course of several weeks by adding a little of the new food to the old food and gradually increasing the amount of new food. If you suddenly change your dog's diet, he can get an upset stomach and you'll have a mess to clean up.

As you can see, there are many choices of foods you can feed your dog. Whatever diet you choose, do your research and make sure you are offering a healthy, balanced diet that meets his needs.

Avoid giving your dog animal bones that can splinter, such as chicken bones or sharp pork chop bones. Some of the main foods dogs should avoid that can lead to toxicity are chocolate, onions, grapes, raisins, macadamia nuts, avocado, coffee, mushrooms, and moldy foods.

While I was working at an animal hospital, several dogs came in as emergencies after eating chocolate. We lost a few wonderful dogs that way, and it was very sad. But one day a Great Dane came in for an emergency after getting into a bag of miniature candy bars. He had eaten the entire five-pound bag of chocolates, with the wrappers still on! Interestingly, those wrappers saved his life—they prevented him from digesting all the chocolates immediately. A lot of people don't know how deadly chocolate can be for dogs. Most of all, it is important to talk with your veterinarian about the details of your dog's food for your particular dog's health.

Spay/Neuter

According to the humane society, millions of dogs are euthanized (killed by lethal injection) each year. Most of these pets don't have anything "wrong" with them but are killed because there just isn't enough space for them. Please do your part to help the overpopulation by having your dog spayed/neutered.

Spaying/neutering can help prevent behavior problems too. A spayed or neutered dog is generally calmer and easier to train, and his focus will be on you instead of on finding a mate. When a dog is intact, he can signal things in other dogs that you won't be aware of, which can cause a lot of problems down the line for you. Unneutered males may spray urine and display mounting behaviors. Unspayed female dogs will have a bloody discharge during their cycle that can be messy for you to clean up, and they attract unwanted male dogs onto your property that may spray strong-smelling urine. Both unneutered males and unspayed females in search of a mate risk getting lost or hit by a car.

Spayed and neutered dogs live longer, are healthier, and even certain forms of cancers are reduced, such as breast cancer in female dogs and testicular cancer in male dogs. The best prevention is spaying females before their first heat and males before the age of six months, according to the ASPCA.

Some more facts, from No Voice Unheard:

- It is believed that unneutered males can smell an intact female from up to 5 miles away! With this in mind it is easy to understand how dogs that are not spayed or neutered may be more likely to wander and become lost.
- Percent of dogs hit by cars that are unneutered males: 80 percent.
- Number of litters a female dog can produce in one year: 2, with an average 8 to 10 puppies per litter. In 6 years, one dog and her offspring can theoretically produce 67,000 dogs.

Spaying/neutering is a routine procedure and dogs recover very quickly from it. Leave breeding to experienced professionals who put a lot of science into keeping the breed healthy. If you are unable to afford the procedure, there are financial assistance programs available. Contact your local humane society and your veterinarian to learn more.

Toys and Bones

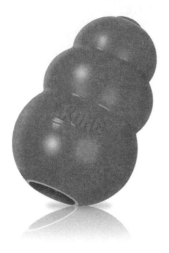

Dogs tend to explore the world with their mouth and like to have something to chew on, so provide chew toys and bones. This also promotes good dental hygiene. But, as a safety precaution, think about what you are offering and make sure it is appropriate for your dog's size and chewing strength, or he can choke on it. Just because a toy or bone is available doesn't mean it is safe for *your* dog.

Strong chewers can chew through just about anything, so supervise them with toys. One of my favorite toys for strong chewers is the Classic KONG that comes in a variety of sizes. I get the extra-large one for Fax because he is big and he could potentially swallow a small one. This toy's unique shape makes it fun to throw for your dog. It bounces all over in unexpected ways when it hits the ground, making it entertaining to try to capture. It even has an opening in the middle that you can put kibble and peanut butter in and freeze so your dog can spend a good portion of his time licking it out. This is great to do when you are having people over and want your dog occupied for a while or if you plan to leave him alone. Check with your veterinarian about what type of filling is appropriate for your dog.

Most toys should be supervised so your dog does not swallow them. If the toy has any string, buttons, or other things that can come off and cause your dog to choke, remove them. (As a rule of thumb, if a toy doesn't look safe for your child to chew, don't give it to your dog.) Rope toys should be used for play only when you are around to supervise and picked up when you aren't. It's a good idea to offer only a couple of toys at a time and rotate them to keep your dog interested.

Talk with your veterinarian about what kind of chew bones are appropriate for your dog. If you are vegetarian and want vegetarian options for your dog, there are several products available.

Crate Training

A crate isn't doggy prison. Many dogs enjoy crates because they feel denlike. A crate is also a good housebreaking tool because dogs do not like to soil in the place they sleep. It is helpful in reducing separation anxiety and destructive chewing, and is great for travel. Many hotels that allow dogs require that they be in a crate when you are away from the room.

Having your dog used to spending time in a crate can be a good thing as long as it is done properly and not abused. The crate should be only positive to a dog, so never discipline your dog by putting him in the crate. He will not understand why you are putting him in there anyway and will start associating the crate with punishment.

LET ME OUT!

Julia, a new client, requested that I come to her home immediately to help with her out-of-control boxer mix, Bruno. She had raised Bruno since he was a puppy and now he was about 1½. When I arrived, Bruno was inside a crate, looking like he was ready to jump out of his skin. Julia worked long hours and when she returned home, Bruno was so frenetic that she would have to put him back in the crate even when she was home. He also slept in the crate at night! Her roommate was scared of Bruno, and Julia felt she couldn't have friends over unless he was in the crate.

I asked Julia to take Bruno out of the crate so that I could get an idea of what she was talking about. Bruno lunged at me like a wild animal, nipping at my hair while jumping uncontrollably all over the kitchen, racing into the living room and all over the furniture, and jumping hysterically at everyone in the room. He was like a jumping bean. Julia's roommate couldn't even be around when Bruno was out of his crate. This was one of the most frantic dogs I had ever seen. Both Julia and her roommate had scratches all over their arms and legs. The furniture was torn up as well.

I asked if Bruno had been getting any exercise. Julia claimed she took him on an hour walk every day but he was still like this. (I wondered if she was being honest.) As I inquired more, I realized that even if Julia was taking Bruno on a walk every day, the rest of the time he stayed inside his crate. He lived almost his whole life inside the crate—day and night. That would make me wild too!

Julia was young, healthy, and active—perfectly capable of exercising her dog. She even mentioned that she went to the gym to work out almost every day. I firmly believe that people who have high-energy dogs should not be at the gym unless they have exercised and spent time with their dogs first. There are so many fun, active things you can do with your dog that can satisfy both your and your dog's exercise requirements.

We decided that this high-energy dog would greatly benefit from staying at doggy day care while Julia was at work during the day. Doggy day care is a great place to bring your dog when you work long hours and have a high-energy dog or a dog who doesn't do well being alone. A good day care is one that lets your dog romp around with other dogs and have much needed attention from humans and plenty of exercise.

We also worked on obedience training. Julia later reported that after attending doggy day care, Bruno was so much happier. He was more in control and the training was going well, so she didn't keep him in the crate so much. I taught her how to train him to greet people in a more calm way and lie down and be relaxed while her friends were visiting. I even included the roommate in some of the training so she could feel more confident living with Bruno.

This story is a good example of how *not* to use a crate. But, when used properly, it can be an enjoyable experience for a dog instead of a torturous one.

If introduced properly, dogs often choose to hang out in their crates even when they don't have to. But dogs should not spend the majority of their time in a crate; it is cruel to keep them in it day and night. Dogs must have proper exercise every day as well.

Pick the Right Crate

Crates come in all different shapes and sizes. The crate should be large enough that the puppy or dog can stand up, turn around, and change positions, but not so large that he has room to walk around and eliminate in it. Many are designed to grow with puppies; they have a partition that you can use to close off part of the crate until they "grow into it." There are different styles of crates, some plastic with little windows and a metal door, others metal wire. If you are using a wire crate, it is a good idea to cover all the sides except the entrance with a blanket or sheet so the crate feels more cozy and secure.

Puppies and Crates

According to the ASPCA, "An 8- to 16-week-old puppy should not be crated for longer than an hour at a time, except during the night." At night, a puppy this age should be taken outside to relieve himself every 2–3 hours. It is also advised that puppies under 9 weeks of age not be crated at all, because they are not able to hold their urine, and you don't want them to begin to soil in their crate and develop a bad habit. Puppies may eliminate up to a dozen times a day! Puppies under 4 months of age have little bladder control. "A four- to six-month-old puppy shouldn't be crated for longer than two to three hours," according to the ASPCA.

INTRODUCING THE CRATE

1. If possible, remove the top of the crate or the door initially. This will make the crate less scary.
2. Remove the dog's collar before having him go inside the crate because you don't want the collar to get caught on something and cause injury.
3. Drop treats or favorite toys in the crate several times a day. Your dog will practice going into the crate to get the treat. It's okay if he comes out again. For now you are just making the whole thing fun. Your dog will start to associate the crate with treats and good things.
4. Never push your dog into the crate. Just throw the treat or toy inside and encourage him to go get it.
5. In the early stages, don't close your dog in the crate. You want him to feel comfortable going in and out on his own right now. Do not force him to stay inside.
6. You may find it helpful to feed your dog inside the crate.
7. Start to give it a name, like "Go inside your crate," and every time you drop the treat inside the crate you say the command. Eventually you will just have to say the command and he'll go inside.
8. Slowly start encouraging your dog to lie down inside the crate. When he goes inside and begins to turn around to come out, encourage him to lie down by holding a treat in your hand. Keep your hand closed and lure him into a lying-down position. The minute he lies down, open your hand and give the treat. Then say "Release" and allow your dog to exit.
9. Practice this often until your dog naturally begins to lie down inside the crate. Treat when he lies down; say "Release" when he exits.
10. When your dog begins to go inside on cue and lies down automatically, begin to make him wait a second for the treat. You want to slowly begin to make him learn to wait for the treat. Build up gradually to 20 seconds. Follow the treat with the release command.

11. When your dog is going into the crate on command and lying down automatically, don't treat him if he goes inside and doesn't lie down. See how your expectations have increased? If he walks inside and comes right out again, no treat. You want to encourage him to lie there for extended periods of time in preparation for being able to close the door soon.

12. When your dog can stay inside of the crate, lying down, for about a minute while patiently waiting for the treat, you can begin to practice with the door. If you haven't already, put the door on without your dog watching. The sound may make him nervous. Now practice your routine, and this time touch the door, then throw a treat inside and release him. You are conditioning him to associate the sound of the door with good things.

13. Next, close the door but don't latch it, and treat and release.

14. When your dog is doing well, close the door and latch it, then treat and release.

15. If your dog scratches or barks to get out, say "No" and lure him with the treat into the down position and then give the treat (try to do this without opening the door). If you let your dog out when he is scratching or barking, you are rewarding that behavior and it will get worse. If you have to open the door to get your dog into a down position, reach in and offer the treat hand as your lure to get him to lie down. Treat and release.

16. If you must open the door when your dog is barking or scratching to get out, you have two options: (1) Encourage him to lie down quietly before you open the crate. (2) Make a loud sound secretly, like slapping the wall, to startle him, and in the second he is wondering what that sound was, open the door. (Be sure he doesn't see you slap the wall; you don't want him to know the noise came from you.) In both cases, you have opened the door when your dog was quiet.

17. If your dog is doing well and you can begin to leave him in there for up to a half hour with no problem, you can gradually increase the time. You can offer a special chew bone or a KONG toy stuffed with treats.

18. At this point you are still in the room with your dog. Now that he is comfortable with the tasty chew bone or stuffed KONG, you can practice getting up and moving toward the door. If he is doing well, you can even practice leaving the room. Come back and praise and try to leave again.

Do . . .

- remove your dog's collar before leaving him in the crate.
- practice gradually and keep things positive and fun.
- make sure your dog has fully eliminated.
- make sure your dog has access to fresh water.

Don't crate your dog if . . .

- he hasn't eliminated fully.
- he hasn't had enough exercise.
- it is too hot.
- he is vomiting or has diarrhea.
- you will be gone more than 5 hours for an adult dog; less for a puppy.

NEVER . . .

- crate your dog in very hot weather in a car or in the sun.

19. You have been spending plenty of quality time with your new pal, so you should be able to tell how quickly you should proceed with any of these steps. If your dog is showing agitation, barking, or scratching to get out, you may have moved too quickly. Practice at your dog's comfort level and very gradually increase.

20. Carefully watch the bedding and toys you leave in the crate. If your dog begins to destroy the bedding, take it out. The toys and bones in the crate should be strong and indestructible.

21. If you discover that your dog has eliminated in the crate, don't punish him after the fact. He won't understand what he did wrong, and this could make him afraid of the crate and/or of you.

Location of the Crate

Locate the crate at first in an area you generally spend time in. If you plan to leave your dog in the crate for more than 2 hours, provide water. For puppies you can use the rabbit-type water dispensers so they don't spill it. First crate your dog while you are home so he doesn't associate the crate with your absence.

It is cruel to crate your dog when you have not sufficiently exercised him beforehand. If the weather is hot, make sure he has cooled down and has cold water before you leave.

If your dog stays in a crate all day and again all night, then it *is* doggy prison.

★ Crate Training Q & A ★

Q I have a very cute and loving 12-week-old Lab, Koby. We brought him home 3 days ago and have been trying to crate train him. He makes a lot of noise when in the crate and last night even started to bark. He is very attached to me since day one and wants to be next to me at all times.

I just read your article about crate training, which is very helpful! However, what I'm struggling to understand is what to do with the dog during the night when he cries and whines if he is not with us in the bed. The last thing we want is for the dog to sleep in our bed! We put the crate in our bedroom hoping that he will feel close to us and sleep, but it's the same story—he doesn't stop crying and whining. We've hardly slept for 3 nights now and I feel like I'm not doing it right and it will affect the dog's behavior.

A The first few days with your new puppy can be a very difficult time. He may be missing his littermates and/or mother, and it can take time for everyone to adjust to the new routines. There are a few things, though, that should make it a little easier for you.

Putting Koby in the crate in your bedroom for the night is a good idea as long as the crate is a positive place for him. Being near you, even if in a crate, is a chance for Koby to bond with you. To use the crate successfully, never punish Koby by putting him into it; you want the crate to feel like a very happy place for your dog.

Some people use a short tether attached to the bed to keep their dog nearby. If Koby is allowed to roam freely in the room, he may have an accident, but if he is tethered to a smaller area he tends to not want to soil his sleeping area.

Do not let Koby sleep in your bed "sometimes." It will confuse him and make your training more difficult. Keep in mind how large he will become!

Dogs learn quickly from routine. Do the same thing the same way every night and he will catch on soon.

Here are tips to get through the night with Koby:

- Make sure he doesn't have any food or water after about 7 P.M., unless the weather is hot.
- Try to keep him awake for 2–3 hours before bedtime. You don't want him to have napped for 3 hours and then be ready to play when you are ready to sleep!

- Tire him out just before bedtime so he will be more likely to sleep.
- The last time you let him outside to eliminate before going to sleep, make sure you give him enough time to fully eliminate and pay attention to what he is doing so you know if he emptied his bladder completely.
- Expect to get up every 2–3 hours to take Koby outside to eliminate.

Crating Your Dog Overnight

At first, many puppies and adult dogs whine when they are in the crate. This can quickly drive you crazy—and break your heart.

Assuming your dog isn't sick and was outside shortly before, it is best to ignore the whining. This is hard to do, but if you give your dog attention at this time, you teach him that whining is a good way to get what he wants, and it will continue. It is better to set firm rules at the beginning. After a night or two of being consistent, your dog will understand that you won't come when he whines.

If your dog (more often a puppy) has been quiet for a few hours and suddenly starts whining, bring him outside to eliminate. Outside, don't play with your dog. Do praise him for eliminating, then take him back to his crate. This is elimination/sleep time, not playtime.

If you want your dog to sleep in his crate, don't leave him in the crate all day. He needs time to wander and explore and sniff and socialize. Also be sure to exercise your dog a lot during the day. A tired dog sleeps well.

With consistency and patience, soon both of you will be getting a good night's sleep.

Housetraining the Adult Dog

Does your dog sometimes pee or poop in the house? This issue is mostly about education and prevention. Puppies and some small breeds cannot physically hold their urine very long, so it is up to you to make sure you are bringing them out very often and observing their urine output. Other dogs who eliminate in the house may be doing it out of habit or may simply need more training.

First, clean all areas that your dog may have messed in and remove the odor with an odor neutralizer from the pet store.

Observe your dog when he is outside peeing or pooping. When he does eliminate outside, praise him enthusiastically. You want him to understand how happy this makes you.

If you do not know for sure that your dog eliminated outside it is hard to know if

> *No matter how small, acknowledge the achievement.*
> *~Greg Henry Quinn~*

he will do so inside, so pay close attention. If your dog pees a lot outside, praise him; he will be okay for another hour or two. If there was just a little urine, bring him back out in a half hour. Give this a name too, like "Do your business" or "Go potty," and make it sound positive. Inside, if your dog is having accidents, I suggest that you have him on-leash attached to you for a couple of weeks so that you can quickly react if there is an accident.

Never Get Angry

If there is an accident say "No" firmly but not in an angry way, then bring your dog outside to pee and praise him while peeing. Never yell at your dog—it will just make things worse. You'll need to watch your dog and catch him in the act. Dogs need to be praised or corrected immediately. Your dog doesn't remember what he did—good or bad—even five seconds ago. You must

> If your dog is submissively urinating, that is a different situation. Read about that on page 157.

say no when he is actually in the process of peeing or pooping. Be very matter-of-fact or you will make the situation worse.

Be vigilant about observing and preventing. If you put the effort in now, it will pay off. Your dog should not have free access to the house until the accidents have stopped completely. Allow him only in the room you are in, and observe closely. If there have been no more accidents in the home for a couple weeks, you can begin to offer more of the house slowly. At this point, it is about prevention on your part to fix the problem.

Being On-lead in the House

The reason for holding your dog on-leash in the house is that you can correct a problem immediately, such as peeing on the floor. Quick reaction time is important. There should not be a problem having your dog on-lead as long as you are watching him and he is not having a reaction to the lead. Better, attach the leash to you, looped to your belt, so he learns to move when you do and do what you do. If you get up to go in another room, he has to go with you; if you sit and rest, he has to rest, etc. This is another way for you to establish yourself as leader with your dog.

Your dog actually likes being on-lead with you because it gives him a job to do. Dogs like to feel busy too, as we do. Their job is to pay attention to your movements. This maximizes bonding as well.

When there have been no accidents in the house for several weeks, you should be able to practice having your dog off-leash again but supervised closely initially. If there is an accident, go back to the beginning and have your dog with you at all times.

It will take a little work initially to have a close watch on your dog, but if you are serious about stopping the problem, this is the road to success. It will be worth the effort when you have a clean house again!

★ Male Dog Marking Territory Q & A ★

Q My dog Buddy is completely housetrained in our home. The problem is he feels a need to mark in other people's homes (and occasionally in places that are sort of gray areas, like garages or patios). He especially marks in houses that have dogs. It's not that he's incontinent or really has to go. I feel he's purposely leaving his calling card.

A It is frustrating—and embarrassing—to be at a friend's house and your dog pees on the furniture! Marking territory is a totally different issue from housetraining. It is an instinctual behavior that dogs use to communicate to other dogs. The scent of their urine lets other dogs know all about them. Some dogs mark their territory out of stress or anxiety, and others to let the dogs in the area know they are here and they may want to dominate this territory.

Since dominance or anxiety issues can be the reason behind the marking, you can sometimes eliminate the problem by working on those issues through a positive-based obedience program.

If it is a dominance issue, you can communicate to Buddy what you expect of him through a positive program, and can often solve the problem. If it is an anxiety issue, positive obedience training can build a dog's confidence and also solve the problem.

Here are suggestions to eliminate the problem:

1. **Neuter.** Studies show that neutering can help stop some male dogs from marking territory.
2. **Begin a positive-based obedience program** so that you can communicate to Buddy what is acceptable and what isn't more effectively.
3. **Use a leash.** Have Buddy on-leash when you socialize and work on catching him in the act to stop the behavior before it starts. Sometimes if you let the rules be known in the beginning, your dog will understand your expectations. Do not punish your dog by hitting him for this kind of behavior (or any other behavior) or you will cause more problems. Positive-based programs are more effective. Watch Buddy carefully and you will become good at spotting his body language *before* he marks so you can stop the behavior easily and without punishment. If you see him about to mark, quickly say "No" and move him away from the spot. Take him out to empty his bladder and watch him carefully when you bring him back in. Be consistent.
4. **Remove all urine odors** with special odor neutralizers. This removes the temptation to mark a spot where he smells urine.
5. **Prevention.** Either keep your dog on-leash with you or confine him to an area that will prevent him from marking when you are not able to watch him.

Puppy 101

Dogs are generally considered puppies up to age 6 months, and from 6 to 18 months they are considered adolescents (teenagers). If you have a puppy, "Puppy 101" will teach you a few basics. If you don't, skip to the next chapter.

Housetraining

Unless you can monitor your puppy 24 hours a day, don't expect to complete the housetraining until your puppy is at least 6 months old. He has not yet developed bowel and bladder control, so he cannot hold urine or feces as long as an adult dog can. Puppies may need to eliminate every hour, so your best bet is to take him out before an accident.

When you have to leave your puppy home alone, confine him to a small, puppy-proofed room and paper the entire floor. Put his bed, toys, and food/water bowls there. Your puppy may play with the papers, chew on them, and drag them around. Don't get upset—this stage will pass. The important thing is that as soon as you get home, clean up the mess and lay down fresh papers.

Eventually your puppy will begin to eliminate on just the paper. When this happens, you can begin to put the paper only in a designated spot and take away some of the extra paper. Your goal is to get him to eliminate on the paper and slowly confine paper in the room to one spot. Don't rush this. Do it at your puppy's pace.

When you are home but can't attend to your puppy, follow these same procedures. However, the more time you spend with your puppy, the quicker he will be housetrained. Your goal is to take your puppy to his designated spot outside every time he needs to eliminate. This should be about every 45 minutes, just after a play session, just after eating or drinking, and right when he wakes up. When your puppy does eliminate in his designated outside area, praise and reward him a lot!

Do *not* get angry at or punish your puppy's mistakes or accidents. He is too young to understand and it can set the housetraining process back drastically. Instead, if your puppy is in the process of eliminating inside, secretly startle him with a loud noise, like stomping on the ground or slapping the wall (don't yell). This will interrupt what he is doing, so you can take him outside. Be sure he doesn't know the noise is coming from you. You don't want your puppy to start to fear you if you are harsh with him for accidents, or he might just go hide and leave you a surprise when you aren't looking.

Here are the steps to follow:

1. Bring your puppy to the place you want him to eliminate and ask him to "Do your business" or "Go potty." Whatever words you use are fine as long as everyone in the household consistently uses them.

2. Be quiet when your puppy is out there and pay attention because when he is just about finished eliminating, you want to praise or treat at that moment.

3. When he has finished eliminating, you can play a few minutes before bringing him back inside.

Your puppy should not be roaming in the house unless he is with you and you know he has just eliminated. It can be a good idea to keep him on-leash at this point so you can quickly bring him outside as needed. It is about prevention. When your puppy has become reliable you can begin offering more freedom in the home. When you cannot supervise your puppy, you must keep him in his enclosed area with the papers on the floor.

If you spend a lot of time with your puppy and reward him for eliminating outside in the designated spot, the process will go a lot faster. Be consistent, calm, and patient. When puppies are older, they can hold it longer.

Accidents are usually the human's fault—allowing too much freedom in the house too soon or not taking the puppy outside enough. With good timing and forethought, you will succeed.

★ Puppy Soiling Bed at Night Q & A ★

Q *I thought dogs don't soil their own beds. Magic, our 10-week-old wire fox terrier, has a crate covered with an old sheet, a heater to keep the room warm, and an appropriate-sized plastic box that has a clean towel in it for comfort. We recognize that puppies are going through a difficult transition period. We let her outside to relieve herself before bedtime. Her water is removed at 7 P.M. She is exercised before bed. Good idea about keeping her up before bedtime, though; I will remember that. In the morning I would expect some soiling in the cage, but her bed is always wet, and twice I have found feces there as well.*

We wash down her cage and her bed and change her bedding each time. What can we do? We have never put any of our dogs in our bedroom, especially uncrated. Magic loves to bolt to the carpet to relieve herself.

A At 10 weeks old, Magic is not capable of staying dry from night through morning. Bring her outside every 2 hours to eliminate. A puppy this age is a lot like a newborn baby. Both require you to get up several times in the night to attend their needs! It can be a lot of work, but it will be worth it in the end. If you don't get up, it will teach Magic that it's okay to soil her bed: That can be a problem later; she may never stop doing it. How long do you have to do this? For every month of age, add one hour. If a puppy is 2 months old, he can go about 2–3 hours before needing to eliminate. It won't be until Magic is about 6 months old that she can wait about 6–7 hours at night. This is tough news if you like a long night of sleep! But it has to be done, so take shifts with your spouse. Pick up Magic, bring her outside to eliminate, praise her, and put her back to sleep. Don't play at this time, just have her do her business and go back to sleep. Time will pass quickly and soon you will be through this difficult puppy stage.

Socializing

Socializing your puppy is one of the most important things you can do. For dogs to live in our human world, we need control over their behavior. If you want an adult dog that is friendly, confident, adaptable, and secure in the world, socializing him well when he's a puppy is the key. Fearful, insecure adult dogs often were not socialized properly as puppies. Socialization can also mean the difference between an adult dog who is aggressive with other dogs and one who understands other dogs' behavior. Socializing teaches your puppy how to handle the world of humans and other dogs.

Introduce your puppy to all kinds of situations—new smells, sounds, people, children, things with wheels, and noisy things. Also expose your puppy to different surfaces, including linoleum floors, cement, dirt, grass, and grates. Introduce new things to your puppy slowly, and make it a positive experience. For example, don't turn on the vacuum right at the moment he sniffs it for the first time. Instead, turn it on when he is in another room, then turn it off and let him come investigate it. Praise him when he sniffs the vacuum. Never drag or push your puppy to explore something he fears. Encourage your puppy to check out unfamiliar things and praise him when he does to build his confidence.

Take your puppy with you to a variety of places. Introduce him to dogs you know are friendly. You want your puppy to get the idea that other dogs can be their friends. Don't bring your puppy to a dog park before he is ready. A lot of bigger dogs running and jumping can be scary. Begin by going to the park when there are only a few other—small—dogs there.

You can enroll your puppy in a good puppy group class so that he has exposure to other dogs in a controlled way.

Puppies go through this important socialization period from about 3–12 weeks old. While it is always important to socialize your puppy, this time is of particular importance. Positive exposures to a variety of things at this age influence how your puppy will turn out. Too much stimulation can cause fear, so introduce things gradually and through positive training. Since you will most likely not get your puppy until they are at least 8 weeks old, be sure to talk to the breeder to find out about what socialization they have provided up to that point.

Between 8 and 10 weeks of age, puppies go through a fear/avoidance stage. It is thought that at this time puppies are becoming acutely aware of all their senses, and a puppy who was extremely confident before suddenly starts acting fearful. Don't worry—this phase should pass. But be careful not to overwhelm your puppy during this period. Take things slowly and make it a positive experience.

Most puppies do not complete their vaccinations until about 16 weeks of age. Some people believe that exposing a puppy to the world before he is fully vaccinated puts him at risk of disease. This may be true, but if you keep your puppy isolated you may end up missing the chance to offer socialization during the time that is so critical. Many people argue that not socializing your puppy before 16 weeks puts him at risk of behavior problems. I have seen this happen. Some people suggest that the risk of death is greater for a dog with behavioral problems due to improper socialization than it is from catching a disease from not being completely vaccinated.

I suggest that if you do decide to take your puppy out before all the vaccinations are complete, avoid areas where other dogs defecate to help minimize your risks. There are many things you can safely expose your puppy to before they are fully vaccinated, including babies, children, wheelchairs, skaters, things with wheels, loud noises, crowds, car rides, strangers petting them, rain, vacuum cleaners, hair dryers, and a drive in the country to smell farm animals. Do research and talk to your vet. Make your choice based on full knowledge of both sides of this issue.

Your puppy should be comfortable being handled. When your puppy is in a relaxed state, give him a gentle full-body rub and get him used to having his whole body touched, including ears, tail, mouth, and legs. It will be a lot less stressful at the veterinarian's if your puppy is used to being handled, plus it allows you to keep a watch on everything to be sure he is healthy.

Q *We adopted a border collie/Lab mix from a "free to good home" ad. She was 6 weeks old when we got her; the original guardians bred the mother and got rid of 6 of her siblings, then abandoned the 4 he couldn't find homes for. We took one of the 4 from the people who rescued them.*

We are worried that since Kit was taken from her mother early she will develop behavior issues later on. Is there anything we should be doing to prevent this? We are socializing her with people and other pets; she is super smart! At 10 weeks she knows how to sit, lie down, come, and go to bed.

A At 10 weeks old, Kit is in the socialization period (3–12 weeks) and also the fear imprint period (8–10 weeks). This is an important time for her. During the fear imprint period it is believed that any traumatic experience can have a lasting impact, so gradually introduce Kit to new things and people. Try to make her experiences positive using praise, toys, and treats.

Don't force Kit into fearful situations; allow her to slowly adjust. You sound like you are already doing obedience, which is fantastic because you are establishing your leadership role. If done well, Kit is learning important respect. At this state she should also be learning bite inhibition from you and through a lot of free playtime with other puppies and friendly adult dogs. If possible, enroll her in a good puppy socialization class.

Introducing Your Puppy to the Leash
This is an easy 2-step process.

Step 1
Get a delicious treat ready that your puppy loves before you put the leash on. Use a standard 6-foot leash. Put the leash on your puppy, give him the treat, and let him drag the

leash around without you holding it. Watch carefully so he doesn't get caught on anything. Let him drag it around for a few minutes, then take it off. Do another session later, gradually extending the time your puppy is wearing the leash. Whenever you put the leash on, give your puppy a yummy treat so he starts to have a positive reaction to the leash. When your puppy feels happy to put the leash on and is used to dragging it around, you can move on to step 2.

Step 2

Put the leash on your puppy and pick up the end. Do not pull on it; instead follow your puppy around. You can encourage him to come toward you with food treats and praise him when he is walking with you. If your puppy sits with the leash on and you want to encourage him to walk, use a food reward and entice him to come with you. Do not pull him toward you with the leash. It is important that he not feel tension on his collar at this point. Keep the experience really pleasant for your puppy and be enthusiastic when he has the leash on. Over time,

> Always do training sessions when you are feeling calm. If you are tired or cranky, your puppy will get signals that you are not happy with him, and the training experience can be confusing. Whenever you feel yourself getting frustrated with your puppy, take a break and begin again when you feel up to it.

you can move away from your puppy, enticing him to come with you and treating him when he does. Eventually, your puppy will understand that when he walks with you, he gets a reward and the walk is fun!

Jumping

Dogs love to jump on each other. That is one way they play together. It is natural behavior for them and they don't know that jumping on people is not appreciated. Unless you train your puppy otherwise, he will continue to jump on you when he grows up.

Here are tricks to stop the behavior.

1. When your puppy jumps on you, walk into him, making contact if necessary, and ask him to sit. When he sits, give him a treat as soon as his rear hits the ground.
2. If your puppy jumps up to receive the treat, do not give it to him. Remember, when you give a treat, you are rewarding the behavior in that second.

3. You can also turn around with your arms folded and your back to your puppy when he tries to jump on you. Be sure that the second all four paws are on the ground, you praise and treat immediately.

If done consistently, your puppy will quickly get the idea that paws on the ground equals attention. If you sometimes pet him for jumping on you, then you'll never resolve the issue and will be working on the problem for years.

Do not show anger toward your puppy for jumping on you by kneeing him in the chest or anything else that could harm him physically. Remember, he is not trying to be bad; he just hasn't learned otherwise yet, so do not physically punish. Additionally, if you don't reward your puppy by giving him praise or treats for sitting or not jumping, you won't resolve it either. Teach him that jumping doesn't get him attention, but paws on the ground or sitting does.

★ Puppy Jumping Q & A ★

Q *Cody is 4 months old and loves people. While he will sit well, etc., he cannot stop himself from jumping when he meets new people when we are out walking. On-leash he strains to greet them and ignores the sit command. He also likes to jump up on us. This is bad, as he is getting bigger and could easily knock someone down. He responds well to treats but ignores them to greet people. We would appreciate any suggestions.*

A In training him to stop jumping, first do training setups before you do the real thing. Here are the steps to follow:

1. Get a few friends to help.
2. Put Cody on collar and leash.
3. Practice walking up to your friends, and when he begins to jump, say "Off" and quickly move him away from the person he wants to greet.
4. Turn around and approach again.
5. If he begins to jump, repeat the off command and move away again. It is *very* impor-

tant that you repeat until he doesn't jump. If you just take him away and don't repeat, he won't learn what you are trying to teach.

6. He loses your attention if he jumps. He gets rewarded through petting when he doesn't jump.

7. It should just take a few times before he understands that all 4 paws must be on the ground to get attention.

8. Praise and petting should not be overenthusiastic so you do not encourage the jumping.

Cody needs to learn that he does not get attention when he jumps. For this to work, it is essential that he *does* get attention and petting when he doesn't jump. Your timing is important. Set this up when you are doing it as a training session and can pay full attention. If you practice this well and consistently, it won't take you too long to teach him that he gets petted only when he isn't jumping.

Make sure you are consistent about petting him when he approaches you or others and is well behaved. This will be his "payment" for not jumping.

Be clear that when he approaches and jumps, he is taken away and doesn't receive

> **Tip:** Don't allow people to pet your puppy when he is jumping. This is tough, but if you stick it out seriously for a couple of weeks he should understand. When you greet people, explain that you are training him.

attention. When he approaches and does not jump, he must receive praise. If he jumps up during the attention, say "Off" and move away and repeat.

Q *Our dog Ozzie is 6 months old and is pretty well trained in many areas. But in the morning (he rises about 6 A.M., so we do too!), if I don't have a chew for him, he jumps on us in our chairs as we try to enjoy our coffee. He won't just sit next to us and let us pet him.*

I understand that he has been in his crate all night and wants attention. I usually sit on the floor with him and pet him and hold a toy for him to chew, just to give him some love/ human contact. Then I try to sit and have coffee, but he jumps up on our chairs wanting continued attention. So far, no amount of "Off" has any effect on Ozzie. He will get off only if I have a chew for him. Is this normal, needing something to keep him occupied, or is he spoiled?

He does the same thing later in the afternoon after he comes home from a 1½-mile woods walk. He is walked about 3 times a day, totaling about 4 miles, and we play fetch daily with him so he is running too. But he can't just lie down or entertain himself. He knows that when we are up and about—cooking, cleaning, etc.—he won't get attention, but when we sit down to read or whatever, he jumps up on us.

If we don't respond to Ozzie's jumping on us and begging for attention, he gets wild, running in circles around the house. We have to ostracize him to the garage—not a cruel punishment as he likes lying on the cool cement floor and has chews out there.

Are chews the only possible entertainment other than us? Ignoring him doesn't work unless he has something like a chew to occupy him.

We love Ozzie, but he is a monster at times.

A Ozzie isn't spoiled—he's smart! He knows when you are tired and tend to give in. When you are sitting trying to relax, it is often easier to give in to him. So what is the answer?

Since jumping on you is the problem, let him know that he will not get any of your attention when he jumps. You say that he "knows" that when you are cooking or standing he won't get any attention. How do you think he "knows" that? You taught him! With consistency you probably taught him over time that he wouldn't get attention then because you were busy; he *learned* he wouldn't get attention so he doesn't jump on you at those times. But since you give him chew bones and attention for jumping on you when you are sitting, he *learned* that he would get attention when you sit. See how smart he is?

You basically have to do the same thing you did to teach him to leave you alone when you are working. Most likely you ignored him. Here are tips.

I suggest doing practice setups, meaning you sit down and pretend you are going to drink your coffee or relax, but with the intention you are really going to do training setups with him. Ozzie needs to have practice learning what your expectations of him are in those moments, so you are going to set it up for him. Once you teach him what your expectations are, be consistent for it to work in the long run. If you give in occasionally, he'll forever keep pestering you to find out when you'll give in again. If he learns from today on it *never* works, then he'll stop.

The best way to teach Ozzie that he won't get attention when you are trying to relax is to ignore him. But if he jumps on you, simply stand up, don't say anything, fold your arms, don't move, and look away. You are signaling that jumping won't get him what he wants. If he sits quietly next to you, praise him to reward the positive behavior. Then sit back down and try again. It shouldn't take too many times for him to understand that he gets attention when he is behaving well and ignored when he isn't.

For this to work, you need to do it *every* time. This is why I have you do practice setups when you are not too tired so you are prepared and ready for the training.

You mention he gets a good amount of exercise. That's wonderful! Depending on his natural energy level, you might have to change your routine a little and exercise him a bit before your morning coffee. It just depends on how much energy he has stored up in the night, but you might relax a little better if he is able to rest calmly after a walk.

He is still a puppy at 6 months, so it is challenging. Keep up the good work.

Bite Inhibition

It is believed that puppies who are not taught at a young age that biting hurts, and isn't allowed, sometimes grow up to be adult dogs who bite. It is important to teach your puppy that human skin is fragile! Puppies usually learn this from their mother or while playing with their littermates and other dogs. But it is important you also work on this as a precaution.

★ Bite Inhibition Q & A ★

Q *We've had a corgi puppy for a week and he's starting to bite our hands and fingers every time we try to pet him or hold him. Sometimes Charlie's mouthing, other times he bites pretty hard. He's 7 weeks old now. What can we do to make him stop, besides giving him toys/bones to chew?*

A It is good you are searching out how to resolve issues early before more problems develop. Puppy biting/mouthing is a normal part of growing up, because all dogs explore their environments with their mouths and because puppies are teething. Just like human babies, puppies have to gnaw and chew on objects to help cut the new teeth through the gums, so make sure you have appropriate chew toys that Charlie can bite on.

Teach Charlie bite inhibition, where he begins to understand how to control his bite so it isn't so hard. This is a learned behavior. Ideally, puppies learn this inhibition by about 3 months of age and no teeth on you at all by 6 months.

When you first begin to teach this, focus first on the pressure of Charlie's bite, then when he is about 6 months old, he should be totally weaned off any teeth on you at all. That includes your clothes and shoelaces.

Here are steps to follow to teach bite inhibition:

1. When he bites too hard, quickly say "Ouch" in a loud, almost yelping sound. Pull your hands away, look away, and don't move. This is so Charlie understands that play will stop when he bites too hard.
2. Next, offer him something he is allowed to chew on. When he takes the chew toy in his mouth, praise him and give him attention.
3. If he again tries to bite you hard, repeat step 1. You may even leave the room if necessary.
4. Reenter the room and try again. If he again bites too hard, leave the room for several minutes.

It is important to reenter and give Charlie another chance and to stop the training on a good note, so keep leaving and reentering as many times as it takes him to get it. If you practice this a lot right away and you are really consistent, he'll learn quickly.

Over time Charlie will begin to understand that hard biting isn't allowed and that he is rewarded with praise as well as a nice chew toy when he doesn't bite you hard. It is a good idea to have your puppy properly socialized too, because he can learn about this while playing with other puppies.

> If you are *not* consistent and allow the mouthing behavior occasionally, he will never learn to stop. But if you decide from this moment on he is not allowed to do it and you follow my steps, you should be successful very quickly.

Two extremely important factors in having a well-behaved puppy are regular daily exercise and a positive obedience program. A positive obedience program will teach him how to control his behavior and also that you are playing a leadership role in his life, which will make him listen to you better. This is also a great tool to use when he is in the overly excited state. If you sense that he is becoming too excited, stand up and begin obedience practice. That will change the mood to a working mode and he'll learn how to focus his energy. When you do the positive obedience with him, he'll receive the attention he seeks through rewards like praise and treats. In this sense you both win: He gets the attention he wants and you get a better-behaved puppy!

Last, do not show anger or frustration with your puppy.

★ Expectations of a New Puppy Q & A ★

Q Crosby is our second golden retriever. Our 13-year-old Bear died last Thanksgiving. Crosby is 14 weeks old. I know it's awfully young to be having high expectations, but I cannot get him to stop biting or pawing me. He appears to be very smart and figures ways around the things you don't want him to do. In short, I don't think he views me as the leader of the pack.

He learns things very quickly—sit, stay, come, not pulling on the leash—and will perform them graciously until he doesn't feel like it anymore.

I have tried a leadership exercise outlined in a dog-training book, in which you place the puppy in a 30-minute down-stay and keep putting him back down when he gets up. It is a complete disaster and ends up with Crosby nipping and pawing me, rolling around the floor, and once he just escaped and tore around the dining room table like crazy.

I feel like this exercise is doing more harm than good and would like another suggestion. We do the one where he sits and I massage his chest, then put him down and side to side, still massaging and talking. He is willing to do that. But I still think he feels like the alpha dog. Am I being too unrealistic for a puppy of this age? We sent Bear to a trainer at 6 months (he was our first dog). I don't want to wait that long with this little guy. Any suggestions?

A I'm sorry for the loss of Bear. Getting a new puppy is a challenge. It is common to forget how your first dog was as a puppy, because after so many years with Bear you became in sync. Crosby may not be as out of control as you think; most puppies start out this way. I don't always use treats when I train adult dogs, but for puppies I do.

I think the 30-minute down-stay is too much too soon for both of you. Try doing smaller, shorter activities until you are both successful. The idea is to build confidence for *both* of you. Get yummy treats and practice obedience. Ask him to do a sit, and then treat. Ask him to lie down, and treat. Begin to work on the come command. Ask Crosby to come to you and treat when he reaches you. Each time you are both feeling good and building confidence.

You can begin the down-stay, but start with 30 seconds and build up slowly over time. Always end your short sessions on a positive where he has been successful and you feel good about it. You can do several short sessions every day. Work it into your routine with him; ask him to perform a command before eating, before receiving affection, before leaving the house, and before entering. If you make it a routine, he *and* you will build your success together.

I also highly suggest that you spend a large portion of the day with Crosby on-leash with you. Attach the lead to your belt. He has to go where you go. If you go into the bathroom, he lies down and waits for you; if you go into the kitchen, he goes with you and waits for you. Treat and praise when Crosby is behaving well. Having him on-lead with you is a great leadership tool and he will learn to respect you. You will bond more as well, and with increased leadership your puppy will like you even more! You can carry the treats with you, so when you stop to look at the computer, for example, you can ask Crosby to lie down and then treat for that. Don't pet your puppy when he is doing something wrong. Give affection only when he is calm and behaving well. If you pet him when he is misbehaving or demanding, you will reward and encourage the behavior that occurred immediately before he was petted.

Regarding treats, use them for the first 2 weeks to a month or so until you develop more confidence together. Give the treats randomly and sometimes replace them with plain affection. Goldens love affection! The idea here is to teach Crosby to perform commands without the treats too. Hold your hand the same way when you have a treat and when you don't, so it is a visual cue too.

It sounds as if you are feeling frustrated. Crosby will pick up on that feeling and see you as a weak leader. Clear your mind, take a deep breath, and practice the obedience in a calm state of mind. If you feel flustered, don't do the training. Wait. Picture your goal in mind before you start the activity, and then you'll have a clear idea of what your expectations are.

★ Overwhelmed Puppy Q & A ★

Q We have two dogs, both female Australian shepherds. Roxie is 1 year old. She is a great dog who loves other dogs. We socialized her a lot as a puppy and she has always been very submissive and playful. I have never seen her even attempt to nip another dog. We put her through puppy school and basic obedience training. We walk her every night at a big off-lead dog park and have done so since she was 12 weeks old. She loves it.

We now have a new puppy. Sydney is 13 weeks of age. She is a pleasure around the house and loves Roxie. They play happily all day. They both also attend doggy day care one day a week and I've been told that they are an absolute pleasure and play well with other dogs. Other dogs visit our home often and we also take Sydney to friends' places and basically everywhere we go, as we did with Roxie.

We know it is very important to expose our new puppy to as many new situations as possible. However, tonight when we took Sydney to the off-lead dog park now that she has had all of her vaccinations, she was very aggressive, attacking other dogs. She was stiff, growling, and trying to bite. We are quite concerned and shocked—we have never seen this behavior in her (or any of our previous dogs, for that matter) so did not know how to act. We have her enrolled in puppy class, but I would like to know what else we can do to nip this behavior in the bud before she turns into an aggressive dog!

A It's good that you have been so diligent about socializing your puppies and know how important that is. No two dogs are alike, though, so it seems to me that your new puppy probably felt pretty overwhelmed by other unknown dogs approaching her. Many people believe that 13 weeks is too young for dogs in an off-leash dog park. Because there are so many different breeds of dogs, all with different personalities, you cannot control which ones approach Sydney. Her response was to keep them away from her. Adult dogs who are well socialized tend to allow puppies a little slack but will let them know what is appropriate dog behavior and what isn't, which is why we like to have puppies meet these types of dogs during this crucial development. Adult dogs who are not well socialized tend to teach puppies bad manners, which can escalate into problem behavior.

For a while, I suggest limiting Sydney's interactions with dogs to just a few known dogs at a time rather than dozens of unknown dogs at a dog park. If she growls, discourage that behavior rather than coddling her. If you pick up Sydney and give her attention after she has just growled, you reward that growling and tell her you liked it, which will, of course, encourage growling in the future and possibly escalate aggression. Instead, say a quick "No!" and later try to socialize Sydney with the dog she growled at in a more controlled environment, one-on-one. Practice positive obedience near that dog. Ask Sydney to sit, and when she performs the command well, offer her a treat. You can slowly work up to being closer to the other dog (who should be on leash).

Do not force Sydney toward another dog or person she seems to want to pull away from. Be patient and give her time.

It's great that Sydney is doing well at doggy day care. Perhaps that situation feels more secure to her, whereas the dog park felt overwhelming.

When Sydney is greeting other dogs on-leash, make sure that her leash is loose; a tight collar can create frustration, which can lead to aggression. Also, make sure that you feel calm and not nervous, or Sydney will sense your discomfort and feel the same way, which can turn the greeting into something negative.

It sounds like you do understand the importance of socializing your puppy well, by introducing her to all kinds of different experiences. Just remember, Sydney is not Roxie, so you have to adjust things accordingly. Keep up the doggie day care. Talk with the instructors of that class ahead of time about your concerns, so they can be on the lookout for the behavior. Also get a feel for how experienced the instructors are at dealing with aggression, so you can make sure you do everything right. If you don't feel confident in the instructors' experience, try to find another day care.

You are on the right path to resolve the issues and you are dedicated. You are a great role model for noticing something about a puppy and doing something to fix it, rather then letting it turn into a problem that will be much harder to resolve as an adult.

3

STEP ONE—GETTING READY FOR OBEDIENCE

Before everything else,
getting ready is the secret to success.
~Henry Ford~

Feeling Stressed or Overwhelmed?

Stress is not what happens to us. It's our response
TO what happens. And RESPONSE is
something we can choose.
~Maureen Killoran~

Why start a chapter about getting ready for obedience with a section about feeling stressed or overwhelmed? In my experience, people who are stressed often have problems with their dogs. Surprisingly, stress of the human and behavior problems of the dog often go hand in hand. Yes, behavior problems of your dog can cause stress, but your personal stress can also cause behavior problems in your dog! The first step in having a well-behaved dog is controlling your stress levels.

Everyone has some stress, but a lot of stress can disrupt your home life and affect your dog in many ways. It can even affect the success of your training. Your dog may also be the source of some of your stress. An out-of-control dog can be a huge source of stress, but there is a solution: Improve the communication between you and your dog, and successfully meet his needs.

Talking things out can sometimes help when you are dealing with stressors. Whenever you need friendly support, just contact me through my Web site and we can talk. The guidance in this book as well as personal support through my Web site can work wonders!

A well-behaved dog can be part of reducing stress levels. Studies in hospitals have shown that a dog just entering a room can lower a patient's blood pressure.

A survey conducted by the American Psychological Association found that one-third of Americans are "living with extreme stress." Up to 50 percent believe stress has affected their health, relationships, and work. Many believe it has gotten worse in the past 5 years. In the survey, 70 percent of people said they had some kind of physical or physiological problem associated with stress, including fatigue, headache, irritability, anger, nervousness, and sleep problems.

According to the American Institute of Stress, the physical symptoms that occur as a result of stress evolved to be useful when the threat was physical, as in the caveman primitive days when there were wild animals and physical battles. Stress causes our heart rate and blood pressure to rise to allow the blood to reach the brain faster to respond more quickly. Blood sugar also rises, to offer more immediate energy.

Although short-term stress can support you to get things done, or act quickly when needed, long-term stress has major health risks. Stress causes the body to release stress hormones, which can have damaging effects. Too many stress hormones for too long can harm the immune system, causing us to get ill more often. Fluctuating hormone levels can cause mood swings and memory problems, and organs can be damaged, making us more susceptible to heart attack and stroke.

Okay, now that you understand how damaging stress can be to your body, how can it affect your dog? Think of stress like a balloon. If we add too much air to the balloon (too much stress in our life), then any small amount of extra air (stress) can cause the balloon to pop (explosion of temper or frustration). If we are walking around with so much stress in our body, any tiny thing our dog does wrong can send us over the edge of frustration. That's what happens when we carry a lot of stress. Something very small happens, and you lose your patience. Whereas, if we were not filled with stress, we'd have room for an additional stressor and our reaction to our dog might not be frustration. You'll have "room" for patience. Make sense? It's like that for everything, really.

One of the first steps toward having a well-behaved dog is to learn how to manage your own stress levels so you can create the extra space for patience. With patience, you can do just about anything. Additionally, if you are managing your stress levels, you have a more focused mind during training and are able to work toward your goals. If you are filled up with stress, you may not be able to clearly see your goals.

It is also very important to notice how your dog reacts to *your* stress. If you are stressed out about life or Fido's behavior, he'll start feeling a little uncertain about you. Your stress, frustration, or anger tends to send a signal to Fido that you are a weak leader with "issues," and he won't feel confident with you. If your dog is not confident in you, he will not listen to you, and your training will start to fall apart.

Now that you understand how important it is to learn to lower your stress level in life and in training, how do you go about it?

- **Exercise** is one of the most successful natural ways of reducing stress. It also is one of the most important factors in having a well-behaved dog. Exercise with your dog, and you *and* your dog will do better! Don't go to the gym and leave him alone. Get out into nature, if you can, with fresh air and sunshine. Pick an exercise that you both enjoy so you'll be more likely to do it. And once you get your dog better behaved, it will be more fun to take him on walks.
- **Simplify your life.** Sit down and write out what causes you stress and ways you can think about reducing those factors. Make a list of things that have to be done and things that can wait. Prioritize, so you can focus on the most important things in your life.
- **Learn relaxation techniques** such as meditation. Meditation can be whatever you want it to be. If you have never done it before, you can start out just by

MY FAVORITE RELAXATION TECHNIQUE

1. Find a quiet place with no distractions. Turn off the phone. Try to remove sounds and other distractions. If you have children who are old enough, or other household members, let them know this is your special quiet time and they should not disturb you.

2. Lie on your back in a comfortable position with your eyes closed. You can lie on the floor or on your bed. (This exercise is also useful if you are having trouble falling asleep, so in that circumstance you can be in your bed. But if you do not want to fall asleep, I suggest you lie on the floor on a mat or rug.) Relax your arms out to the side or, if you prefer, you can rest your hands on your chest, feeling your breath as you inhale and exhale. Your legs are about hip width apart.

3. Start to focus on your breathing, taking deep breaths in through your nose and out through your mouth. When thoughts start to enter your mind, push them aside and begin again to focus only on your breathing.

4. Now start to concentrate on specific parts of your body with the intention of relaxing them completely, beginning with your eyes.

5. Notice how relaxed your eyes are as they rest in their sockets. You feel the tension begin to leave your face.

6. Turn your attention to your hands. Feel each finger relaxing. Imagine the pulse of your blood flowing all the way to your fingertips.

7. Think of an imaginary line that goes through your whole body and erases the tension. Move from your hands now to your arms. All tension is erased in your arms as you focus on how relaxed you feel.

8. The imaginary line continues to your neck and chest. Take notice of your chest as it rises and falls while you breathe normally. Your body is filling with oxygen and all is as it should be. The tension in your neck fades away as your shoulders melt into the floor or bed below you.

9. Your breath flows easily as your imaginary line travels down through the core of your body. You envision your appreciation for all your organs as they are working in unison to keep you healthy and your body running smoothly.

10. Your lower back melts into the surface below you. Your body is becoming one with the earth and the nature that surrounds you.
11. The line continues to erase all tension as it moves down into your legs and through your feet to your toes. The blood from your heart and oxygen from your poetic breathing flow through your body, and you are now in a state of total relaxation.
12. Lie here as long as you want. Focusing on your breath whenever you feel your mind wonder.

If you get good at this, you will be astonished how it feels. Try to increase the amount of time you can do it every day. Meditation can feel like you just had an hour massage. I practice this whenever I am nervous about something. This is a great tool if you sense you are beginning to feel frustrated or losing your patience with your dog. Focus on the breathing to keep yourself relaxed when needed.

spending a couple minutes out of every day sitting quietly. Focus on your breathing and try not to think about anything for a few minutes. For some, it can help to hum, chant, or listen to special relaxation music to focus on the sound. But the basic idea is that you take a few minutes out of every day to sit and quiet your mind and body.

When you learn to quiet your mind, you will notice that it carries over to the rest of your life. It is like training your brain to be calm. People who meditate regularly can focus easier, and when faced with stressful moments in the day they are more likely to handle them better because they have been "training" their brain. Everything takes practice and training to be good. Make a commitment to relaxing a few minutes every day. Soon, you will "train" yourself to relax, and your dog will improve too. When you are calm, your dog becomes calmer.

- **Write down your thoughts.** Sometimes writing out your thoughts and feelings about things helps keep them in perspective. When you write down something and read it back to yourself, you often see your problem or stress in a whole new way.

- **Take time for yourself.** Listen to music, read a book, take a hot bath. Treat yourself once in a while to something that makes you feel happy and calm. Rejuvenate yourself so you can be a better mother, father, husband, wife, friend, and dog trainer.
- **Be healthy.** Take care of your health. Eat whole grains, fruits, and vegetables and healthy proteins. Skip the junk food and caffeine. Get enough sleep and exercise regularly. Good health is one of the most important factors in leading a happy life. Your body does a lot for you, so make sure you treat it well.
- **Be positive.** Take care of your mental health too. Sometimes, if you tell yourself negative things, they come true, so try to maintain a positive attitude. Don't think negative thoughts about yourself. Be more positive. Love yourself. Your dog will also see that you are more confident, which will make the training go better.
- **Talk it out.** If you have a close friend, family member, or even a counselor or psychologist whom you can share with, it can help you destress to talk things out. Sometimes the act of talking about your stress can actually decrease it, like a form of release.
- **Contact Julie.** If you want to talk about your dog or any other stressors, contact me at www.webDogTrainer.com.

I am optimistic that you can live a healthier, happier life with your dog. Learning how to manage your stress will help you cope with whatever comes your way. If you are happier, your dog will be happier. You will feel better, stronger, and more focused during your training. Your dog will also trust you more, which will make your training flow well.

The Significance of Obedience

The human world is a pretty complicated place for dogs, and a lot of the things they do in their natural world you don't want them to do in yours. Dogs in the wild often leap all over each other in greetings, which is why dogs have that tendency to jump on you when they are excited. But this behavior doesn't work for you, especially if you have a big dog. In the wild, some dogs urinate to show the other dog they recognize his dominance. That's natural in their world, but not on your new carpet.

There are a lot of things in the human world that are not normal in the dog world. Dogs normally explore the world and don't do well staying in one place all day. They are not left alone for long periods of time in nature because they normally live among other dogs in groups. Therefore, it is understandable that your dog will do best if you can try to match his "normal" environment as much as possible in your human world. That involves lots of exercise, new sights and smells, less time alone and more time with you, time to play with his dog pals, and an environment with a calm, clear, natural leader with rules that are consistent so he can understand them.

Dogs in an environment more like their natural one do better and have fewer behavior problems.

We all have busy lives and it's hard to fit a dog's needs into our schedule. However, if you don't make adjustments, essentially you create more problems for yourself. Skipping the daily walks might feel like it gives you more time, but you risk returning to a shredded couch or an unhappy neighbor who listened to barking all day.

If you have physical limitations that prevent you from walking your dog, be a little creative. Hire a professional dog walker or a teen in the neighborhood to walk your dog, or put your dog into doggy day care. Or think about a motorized wheelchair. If the weather is bad outside, your dog can use a treadmill (this takes practice, but your dog will come to love it).

If you think about it, every need of your dog's is actually good for you. He needs exercise and so do you; he needs time with you, and you need his loving companionship. The one creature happiest to see you when you get home is your dog! There is nothing like having a dog offer never-ending love for you. He needs to get out and explore new sights and sounds, so take a trip to the park. You'll both make new friends.

So how exactly do you communicate your human needs to your dog? By teaching him obedience! Obedience is more than just teaching your dog to sit, lie down, or come when called. It is a way to actually communicate with your dog. Even if you do not plan on showing your dog in a competition, teaching him obedience is valuable in many other ways.

Jumping can be controlled through obedience. And since you know that dogs listen to their "leader" in nature, you've learned that if your dog considers you his leader, he will listen to you. Obedience accomplishes that.

People who practice obedience with their dog are leaders in their dog's eyes. This means that your dog respects your judgment and wants to do what you ask him to do. It also means he loves you more! This is important. Some people fear that using obedience with their dog is unkind in some way. But positive-based obedience techniques, like the ones described in this book, are actually fun. When obedience is done well, dogs feel good about themselves because you are giving them sincere praise and reward for accomplishing something. This makes your dog happier *and* teaches him what you'd like him to do.

Obedience can teach your dog to replace behaviors you don't want with ones you do. Instead of jumping on guests when they arrive, your dog can learn to sit happily and receive their attention that way, because you taught him that.

Nothing in dog training happens instantly. It takes practice, but it is worth every minute you put into it. Your dog will be happier, because a better-behaved dog gets to spend more time with you. You'll be happier because you'll know how to control your dog's behaviors in a way that works for everyone. Wouldn't it be fun to go to the off-leash park with your dog or go camping without a leash and feel confident your dog will stay near you and come when called? This is accomplished through obedience. Or maybe you live in a city and want to pass by other dogs and sit calmly with a friend at an outdoor café while your dog happily lies next to you. This is also possible through obedience.

Obedience takes practice and, most important, it takes consistency. If you are clear with your dog and ask the same thing of him every time, he'll learn really quickly. But if you sometimes allow him to jump on you when you are too tired to stop it, and other times you get angry and yell at him to stop, you create confusion—sometimes he can jump and sometimes he can't. But if you make a clear rule that jumping on you is never allowed, your dog will learn it quickly and stop doing it.

> The more inconsistent you are with your dog, the more inconsistent he will be with you.

I believe that if you understand *why* you should do something, you are more likely to do it consistently. My goal throughout this book is to teach you why you should do one thing but not the other. Once you are consistent, learn my techniques, practice your timing, and praise genuinely, you'll discover a marvelous thing: Your dog listens to you!

Being a Calm, Clear, Consistent Leader

In nature, dogs live in groups. The leader is the confident, strong one. The other dogs follow the guidelines of the leader by watching him closely, observing his body language and behavior. The leader teaches them what kind of behavior is acceptable and what are the rules of the group. It helps to understand your dog's mind if you want success in training him. It is natural for a dog to need a leader to help him navigate the complicated human world. If you are not a calm, clear, consistent leader, your human world can be a very stressful place for your dog.

Being the leader means being calm, clear, and consistent always.

- Being calm means you do not express anger, frustration, or anxiety toward your dog.
- Being clear means your dog understands exactly what the rules are.
- Being consistent means you have the same expectations of your dog every day and you follow through with your expectations of your dog, every time.

When you are not calm, clear, and consistent, your dog may not come to you when called, may pull on his leash, not stay consistently, jump up on you or others, or just generally not have desirable, "obedient" behavior. In order to have a calm, consistent dog, you must first be calm, clear, and consistent. Without this understanding between you and your dog, you will not achieve the results you want.

Your dog reads you: He knows if you are hesitant and uncertain or secure and confident. A hesitant, uncertain leader isn't trusted; a secure, confident leader is valued and trusted.

When your dog demands something from you and you give in, you are not being a good leader. Part of being a good leader is setting clear rules for your dog, and jumping up to meet his every need is not one of them. If your dog barks for food, ignore him and do not give it until he is calm. If your dog wants to go in and out often to chase the squirrels in the backyard and you let him in and out at every demand, you are not being a strong leader. If you do want to let him out when he demands it, have him sit first; that way you are still in control of the decision.

What Happens When You Are Not Calm?

Ellen, one of my first clients, had a German shepherd, Bowser, who was high energy and difficult for her to control. She had been to obedience school with Bowser and was quite good at commands inside her home when there weren't any distractions. But on walks, or even in her backyard, Bowser would spot a cat or squirrel and, in her words, "go crazy."

One of the first things I did was observe Ellen walking Bowser. Right away, I noticed Ellen's anxiety and nervous nature. During the walk it just got worse. She could barely hold on to Bowser, and when he spotted a cat, he barked and lunged to such a high level Ellen almost fell down.

I decided to take Bowser's leash and try something. Almost right away I had him in a down-stay with the cat just a few feet away. Ellen was amazed. I wasn't doing that to show off; it was an example of what Bowser was capable of with calm leadership. Ellen tended to be anxious, because she felt she didn't have control on walks with her dog, making her a weak leader, and Bowser observed that nervousness. But when someone like me, who is calm, clear, and consistent, stepped in, Bowser performed beautifully. This is a great example of how the energy you project to your dog affects him and changes the way he behaves.

When Ellen observed her dog's true abilities, she became focused on managing her anxiety with her dog. Every time she lost her calm state, Bowser went back to being uncontrollable. On sessions together I often stopped her and had her take deep, calming breaths to relax before proceeding. Over time, Ellen learned how to control her anxiety and become a calm, clear, consistent leader, and she and Bowser were a lot happier together!

Mark, another client, was interested in bringing his rottweiler Martha to a higher level of obedience. He had already trained her well, but there was a problem area near his house, with a lot of dogs barking on the other side of the fences. Mark and Martha passed that area every day to go to the park. Mark told me that the dogs on the other side of the fences frantically barked, trying to fence-fight Martha whenever they passed by. I went with them one day to observe the hysteria. Mark was right; Martha did great on the walk until passing that section of the neighborhood. When Mark and Martha walked by the frenzy of dogs, Martha would lose control and Mark could barely hold on to her. The daily walks had become a stressful event for both of them.

I observed Mark's body language. He noticeably tensed up when they approached that part of the neighborhood. Martha would pick up on that tension and emit a signal to the dogs waiting on the other side of the fences, which would start them all barking. I made Mark aware of this and coached him to be calm and relaxed with a loose leash and walk confidently into that neighborhood with the mind-set of a strong leader. You couldn't believe the difference. The dogs on the other side were quiet! Mark was in shock at how such a small change in his own behavior caused the ricochet effect throughout the neighborhood.

Mark called a few weeks later to report that he and Martha walked past that neighborhood of dogs every day now without stress or hesitation. His wife was also able to walk there, pushing their child in the stroller without worry.

There is a lot going on with dogs and signals that we don't fully understand. But they are very in tune with us and with other dogs. Your nervous, anxious, frustrated, or angry signals toward your dog affect him and make life harder for both of you. When you can approach situations with your dog with calm, clear, consistent leadership, you will see a change right away.

Your dog has to work hard when there are no clear rules. He doesn't know what to do and that can be very stressful for him. Your dog will feel more secure and happier and will love you more when there are set rules to follow. Being too lenient and letting him get away with bad behavior does not work in the long run. Without a clear and consistent leader, one of two things may happen: Problem behavior may develop, or he may break down and become fearful. A fearful dog is not happy.

> Establishing yourself as a calm, clear, consistent leader is the best gift you can give your dog. He will love you more and be happier.

Leadership Rules

The first way to become leader is to establish rules at home for your dog. Here are examples of rules:

- You control the house; your dog doesn't. If he is on the couch or bed and you want him off, it should be easy to accomplish this.

- If someone comes to the door and your dog barks then you should be able to stop the barking.
- If a guest enters the house, your dogs should not bark or jump on her.
- Your dog is not allowed to nip or bite or growl at you. Your dog's teeth are not allowed on you at any time, even during play.
- If you have food on the counter, your dog should not take it.
- Your dog should understand which toys are his and what things he is not allowed to chew (his chew toy good, remote bad).
- Do not allow your dog to beg for food. Establish a clear area where your dog should be when you eat and stick with that spot every time. Everyone in the household, including the kids, should follow all these rules.
- When it is your dog's turn to eat, he is not allowed to bark or jump all over you while you prepare and serve his food. He should wait, sitting quietly, and only then do you put down his food bowl. If you put the food bowl down while he is barking, you have just rewarded that behavior. You should also be allowed to take the food away or reach into the food bowl whenever you want.
- This is true for treats and toys as well. You own everything and can take it away and give it back without any problem.

It is possible for your dog to easily follow all these rules and many more. Remember, he will be happy to know what is expected of him!

Consistency is very important. If you are clear only 90 percent of the time, that extra 10 percent is enough to confuse your dog about what is expected. For example, if you occasionally allow your dog to jump on certain guests as a greeting but expect him not to jump on others, that is unfair and inconsistent—you will be working on this behavior forever.

Dogs understand only very clear rules that are black and white. They do not understand the gray areas of rules like humans do, or the subtlety of hidden rules. If you are clear in your rules and consistent in your expectation of these house rules, you will have a happy, well-trained dog.

There can be more than one human leader. In fact, all the humans in the household, even the children, must be calm, clear, consistent leaders and agree on the same rules and expectations of your dog. One person should not have different expectations from another. But suppose your daughter likes Snoopy to sleep on her bed whereas you want only human animals on your bed. If you have taught Snoopy which furniture is okay and which is off-limits that works too, as long as you are consistent.

> Set your rules, make them clear, and stick to them.

Train your dog well so that you can take him with you to explore the world, whether it is on a hike in the mountains or a trip down the sidewalk. Dogs don't like to be cooped up in the house any more than you do.

It is a beautiful experience to have a well-trained dog. You *can* have a dog who is happy, listens to you, and can go wherever you go. You *can* be one of those people others envy because your dog listens to you and doesn't pull you down the street and comes when called. There is so much potential in each and every dog. Open the lines of communication in the way your dog can understand. It is possible and I know you can do it!

You can love and hug and kiss your dog as the leader. Understand that there is a time to do that and a time not to. If your dog is behaving in a way you like, you can reward him with your love and attention. Here are examples of when you should *not* give loving attention to your dog:

- He is jumping all over everyone. Do not reward that behavior by petting him.
- He is showing fear. Humans think it is comforting to pet a dog when he is scared, but it in fact reinforces the fear.

Soon the rules will become second nature to you—and your dog. Say it is your dinnertime and you've already established where your dog belongs. You can just point to the area and say "Go to your bed" (or whatever name you have given the area) and he'll go. Your dog really does want to please you, and it is just a matter of making it clear how.

Obedience training is the next step toward being the leader. Obedience training is a tool used to teach dogs things like sit, down, stay, come, etc. I also think of it a bit like teaching a language that both you and your dog will understand. When your dog is taught these things correctly—and, yes, there is a right way and a wrong way—he will understand what you want and obey you happily.

If you learn the proper techniques, your dog will respond consistently to what you ask, and will be happier in general, whether off-leash or on. If done improperly or inconsistently, you'll just confuse your dog. Follow this program closely to perfect these techniques and have reliable results.

EXERCISE, EXERCISE, EXERCISE your dog! You will not have success in any area of your training if your dog doesn't get enough *daily*. He needs to drain all his energy. The number one rule of good dog behavior: A tired dog is a good dog. Plus, your dog wants to walk and run and play outdoors. I will show you how to have a controlled walk with your dog and what type of exercise is right (and enough) for him in the section on exercise (page 80).

Goals

When you know what you want, and want it bad enough,
you will find a way to get it.
~Jim Rohn~

Do you know what you want? Do you know how to get it? Plan for what you want by first writing down your goal, then start writing down your plan toward how you are going to achieve it.

As a private trainer, I have had the benefit of working individually with people. I always ask them what are their own personal goals. This is a very important first step in dog training. For example, do you let Spot on the couch or not? If you don't really care, you are more likely to allow Spot on the couch in the future. Don't bother to "train" him to stay off the couch if it isn't something important enough to you that you would be consistent with it. Instead, put your energy into the things that are very important to you and you would be consistent about. Choose your personal goals and match them to those of other household members.

Determine your training goals based on what is important to you and your family. Also look deep inside yourself and decide if you will be consistent to match that goal. For example, when you are training Spot not to jump on you, you cannot allow him to jump on you *ever*. If one day you are too tired to train Spot and you allow him to jump on you, you have been inconsistent. Why does that matter? You just taught Spot also to be inconsistent. All the training you did do to stop the jumping has now been discredited in his mind.

What are your goals for your dog? List them here:

Example 1: *My dog will sit quietly before I feed him.*

_____

Example 2: *My dog will lie on his special mat nearby while the family eats.*

_____

Example 3: *I will walk my dog for 30 minutes before going to work and for an hour when I return home.*

_____

_____

_____

_____

_____

_____

_____

Understanding Your Dog's Levels of Energy

There are diverse levels of dog energy and at any given moment your dog can display more or less energy based on many factors. Has he been walked recently? Are you being a weak leader? I rate dog energy on a scale of 1 to 10.

Level-1 energy is close to asleep and very relaxed. A dog at level 10 is completely out of control. You have to first drain his energy with exercise to bring the level down to a point where your dog can focus on you.

My client Peter and his German shepherd, Archie, were meeting me at a park for our first session. When Archie got out of the car, he was at level 10. Peter could hardly hold on to him. Archie had reached an overly frantic state and no one could train him in that moment. How did Archie get to level 10? What can Peter do to bring his level down enough to train him?

I asked Peter, "When was the last time you took Archie for a walk?" His reply was, "About a week ago." This typically high-energy GSD's energy had been building up for a week, and when he spotted an open park with people and other dogs he had an explosion of pent-up energy. Who could blame him?

The very first thing we had to do before we could even attempt a training session was to release that pent-up energy through exercise. It took quite some time, but we kept moving, and eventually Archie was calm enough to listen to commands.

Without draining Archie's energy, it would have been like trying to teach quantum physics to a child in the middle of a tantrum. When a dog is at level 10, no one can get him to listen and respond to commands. It's like deflating a balloon; Archie's balloon was so full he was ready to pop if his energy wasn't released. There could have been disastrous results, like aggression toward any nearby child, adult, or other dog.

If your dog doesn't get to release his stored-up energy with *daily* outings, over time that saved energy builds up, ready to explode.

BENEFITS OF EXERCISE

- If you are having guests and you want Lassie calm during the visit, exercise him to wear him out *before* the guests arrive. His natural energy level will be reduced and his behavior will improve.
- You like to bring Lassie to the dog park, but he goes a little crazy when you get close. Exercise him *on the way to* the park. Then Lassie enters at level 5 rather than level 10.
- You want to take Lassie to an outdoor event where there will be a lot of people and other dogs. Exercise him *first* and he'll be much easier to handle.

Even if your dog is properly exercised, it is still possible for him to reach level 10, but he will not *start* at level 10. That means there is a buildup to reach that high level, and as a good handler you can stop the buildup. Many dogs have something that sets them off and leads to level 10, but if you are good at reading your dog you will be able to prevent his energy level from escalating.

Here's an example. Your dog is walking along next to you nicely with no problems and you are both enjoying the walk. Then you notice your dog become agitated and focus intensely on a squirrel. You know your dog has a problem with squirrels and wants to chase them. What do you do? Should you continue on your walk and try to get past that squirrel as fast as you can? No, because the next time your dog sees a squirrel you'll have the same problem.

So what's the solution?

Here is where learning your dog's body language comes in. Dogs generally do not jump from level 3 to 10; it is a process that can be stopped. When you notice the change in your dog, work quickly to gain his focus back onto you with obedience. Ask your dog to sit or lie down, for example. The key is to stop your dog focusing on the squirrel and start focusing on you. If your dog maintains focus on the squirrel, he will reach level 10 and you won't be able to stop it. Change his focus to you.

> *Avoid problems and you'll never be the one who overcame them.*
> *~Richard Bach~*

If you do obedience with your dog facing the distraction and he still cannot take his eyes off it, have him go in a down position with the object behind him so he cannot watch it, and tell him to stay. If it is still difficult to get your dog's attention, move a distance away from the distraction until you can regain his focus.

Do not give in to your dog's desire to watch the object. This is where your leadership comes in. Your dog should do what you want him to do. If you do this successfully, you will instantly see your dog's energy begin to lessen. Because you've put the focus back on to you as the leader, you will have control of your dog and can proceed with the walk. This goes for any major distraction that affects your dog in a way that makes him lose control. I call this the epicenter, the most intense situation that causes your dog to lose it. When those things happen, follow the steps I discussed above to change it. Read on to learn how to do the commands successfully. (I suggest coming back to this chapter after you have read the rest of the book.)

If you are not able to gain control of your dog, you are too close to the epicenter, so move away from it. This can be anywhere from a few feet to a block away. Move away until you notice your dog becoming more relaxed and not focused on the distraction that started it all. Then, after you get control over your dog, slowly and confidently go back toward the epicenter. Go as close as you can just before the control is lost. Practice this as long as you have the energy and drive to do so. It is okay if you do not get directly next to the distraction right now. Continue working on it for a period of time until you do. You may need to work on this daily for weeks or even months. Remember, you and your dog already ought to be good at obedience to work on this kind of distraction right now.

If you are still in the early stages of learning the obedience, do not attempt to get too close to these major distractions yet until your confidence builds. Each time you practice getting close to this distraction makes it easier the next time. It is really about teaching your dog that *he* can be in control when he is near big distractions. And, also important, it teaches you that *you* can have control over the situation too. Keep practicing. Don't get discouraged. You should work on major distractions only when you feel calm and confident, never when you feel frustrated. Take a deep breath and relax a bit before you start!

Exercise!

When a dog doesn't get enough exercise or enough energy drained, he can experience many different kinds of problems. Think of it like this: Every dog has a certain amount of energy, and when that energy is not drained, it will come out in ways you do not want, like aggression, separation anxiety, barking, jumping all over—generally being too much to handle. If you want to have a happy and well-behaved dog, the very first step is to drain his energy *every day.* This is essential. Almost every single dog who has come to me with behavioral problems had too much energy stored and not enough of it released.

Dogs Need You to Exercise Them

Dogs actually don't exercise themselves without human direction, even when they have the space to do so. Just having a big backyard is not going to meet your dog's exercise needs. He needs you to guide him to do the exercise.

Dogs Must Leave the House

Imagine how you'd feel if you never left the house. You'd go crazy too! Your dog needs to go outside and experience the world with you. A short stroll down the same street and back is not enough. Dogs must explore new sights and smells and be worn out. How do you know how much energy your dog needs drained?

Take your dog on at least a 30- to 45-minute walk twice a day. Senior dogs, puppies, and toy breeds may need less and high-energy dogs may need more. Talk with your veterinarian about what is right for your dog.

Your Goal Is to Get Your Dog Tired Out

Base the intensity of your exercise on your dog's energy needs. How do you know if it is enough? When you are on your way home from your walk, does your dog drag a bit behind you? When you get home, does he immediately lie down? Then you know he's tired. Success! If you are on your way home and your dog has as much energy as he did at the start of the walk, then obviously it isn't enough. Or if you get home and he is still full of energy, it is not enough. Your dog should feel tired and go lie down when you get home.

For Medium to Large Dogs, Buy a Dog Backpack!

Dog backpacks are specifically designed for use by fully grown, healthy adult dogs that are medium to large size. The straps should be snug, but you should be able to insert one to two fingers between them and your dog. Check the strap when he is standing, sitting, and lying down. The backpack should be large enough to carry the load and at the same time your dog should be able to lie down when wearing it.

Add weight to the backpack that your dog will carry and thus feel more tired. Go on a hike wearing a backpack and you'll see how much more tired you are than when you don't wear it! Ask your veterinarian, but generally you can put in about 10–25 percent of your dog's body weight. For example, a 60-pound dog can carry about 6 pounds, depending on energy level and age. Gauge it by your own dog. Distribute the weight evenly on both sides of the backpack. You can use anything you want; I suggest your dog's favorite ball and maybe a Frisbee, and water and snacks for both of you.

There is another benefit to using a dog backpack. Dogs love to have a job to do in their life. They feel important and proud, and the backpack is a symbol. A lot of my clients have commented that their dogs are almost prancing when they have the backpack on. It is similar to guide dogs and search-and-rescue dogs. They get so excited, wagging their tails, when the harness or pack is put on them. They are performing an essential duty and they love it!

The other benefit, besides draining their energy and making them feel proud, is that dogs usually can concentrate intensely only on one thing, so when they wear the backpack they tend to have a more focused walk. Dogs who generally try to sniff and pull on a walk are more likely to walk in a controlled manner when wearing a backpack. They are focused on the extra weight they are carrying and on balancing the pack.

Some dogs feel a little odd when you first put the backpack on and may show physical signs that they feel uncomfortable, like balking or lying down. Don't worry. Just be positive about it and start moving. Your dog should be fine within a few minutes.

Of course you want to talk to your veterinarian to determine that your dog is healthy and strong enough to wear a backpack. You can use an empty backpack at first, and when your dog gets used to it, gradually add weight. You can also use treats to create a positive experience.

Put Your Dog on a Treadmill

A treadmill is a wonderful tool for draining your dog's energy, especially when the weather keeps you indoors. Your walk with your dog is still important and a treadmill is not a substitute; it's an addition.

When introducing your dog to the treadmill, put his leash and collar on and guide him up onto the treadmill when it is *not* moving. Give him a treat when he is standing on it; do this several times until your dog feels totally comfortable standing on it. Repeat the process and give it a name, like "Hop up." Practice having your dog go on and off several times before you start the treadmill. Now you can start the treadmill *very* slowly while he is standing on it. Your dog may be surprised and jump off. Keep trying until he realizes he can walk on it. When he gets very good at it, increase the speed. Most dogs enjoy this and eventually jump right on!

> Dogs younger than 1½ years of age may not have fully developed bones and joints so running may not be good for them. Always talk with your veterinarian about what is right for your dog.

Collars and Leashes

There are many different types of collars, and choosing the right one can be confusing. To help sort it all out, I've listed some excellent choices.

Flat or Rolled Neck Collar

The traditional cotton or nylon buckle, or quick-release, collar, is a good everyday collar you can hang your dog's ID tags from. It does not tighten on the dog's neck once it is fastened, and many people find that the rolled variety seems to cause less hair breakage. If your dog tends to pull on leash, however, you do *not* want to use this type of collar for walking.

Break-away Collar

This is similar to the flat or rolled neck collar, but if a break-away collar becomes caught on something, it breaks open and releases your dog.

Head Collar and Body Harness

If your dog is strong and pulls on his leash, a head collar is a great idea. Some people use this as their everyday walking collar and some use it until they have trained their dog not to pull. This is a kinder, more effective collar for a serious puller. When you have control over your dog's head, you have control over his whole body. It is similar to the idea of the horse halter. It may look a bit like a muzzle, but it isn't. Your dog can open his mouth and bark, drink, and eat with this collar.

The Gentle Leader (see photo) and the Halti head collars both have a hook that attaches the leash under the chin. Their design is slightly different and preference seems to depend on your dog. Dogs with long snouts, such as German shepherds and collies can wear either. Dogs with shorter snouts, such as boxers, may do better with the Gentle Leader.

If your dog wears a head collar that attaches under the chin, take care that he doesn't jerk his head through the leash or he can get hurt. Do not use retractable leashes with head collars, because when the dog gets to the end of the leash it can accidentally jerk his head.

The Canny collar is similar to the Gentle Leader and Halti. It too has a strap that goes around the dog's snout, but the leash attaches behind your dog's neck rather than under his chin. There are pros and cons to this. The good thing about attaching the leash behind the head is you have less chance of accidentally jerking your dog's head. But some people say that not having their dog's leash attached under the chin gives them less control over heavy pullers. Therefore, heavy, strong pullers may do best with the Gentle Leader or Halti.

There are strong arguments for each type of collar. Your choice depends on the strength of your dog's pull, how the collar fits on his head, and just personal preference.

If possible, try them all and pick your favorite, or even alternate between them. As new collars are invented along the way, I will try to keep you updated through my Web site regarding what is available and what people are saying about them. I'd love to hear from you on what your favorite collar is and why. Your input can help others.

A body harness is worn around your dog's body (see photo). Like the head collar, it does not put pressure on the neck. This is good for puppies, small dogs, and dogs like pugs and bulldogs who have short muzzles and cannot fit a head collar around their snout.

You should try to train your dog to heel and walk without pulling. This takes work, but the reward is worth it. Since training a good heel takes time, a head collar or body harness is a good short-term solution until your dog learns to heel. If you just want a quick no-pull solution and do not plan on working on the heel, it is okay to use a head collar or body harness for your everyday walks.

Introducing a Head Collar to Your Dog

Most dogs try to remove it when you initially put it on, and they can put quite a show on to get it off. But they get used to it rather quickly when introduced to it correctly, and it is a bit of a miracle how easy they are to walk with one!

To introduce it, offer treats to create a positive experience and just keep moving. If you stop, your dog may try to take it off with his paws. Stop your dog from removing it and then keep moving. Usually your dog will forget about it when he begins to enjoy his walk. Occasionally, a dog takes longer to get used to it and will do about anything to get it off. Make sure it is on correctly and then stick with it. Just stop him from removing it and keep moving. It is worth the effort in the long run because it is a wonderful walking tool! Keep in mind that it isn't hurting your dog—it's just a new sensation.

Once you get the fit right, go for a walk. Expect your dog to buck like a horse, tear at it with his paws, rub on your leg to get it off—this is all common behavior at first. He is not used to the feeling yet. Use the leadership skills you've been developing to let him know he does not have the choice to take it off. Your goal on the first walk is to keep him moving (sometimes jogging can help for the first couple times). *Every time* he tries to remove it, quickly stop him with a stern, commanding sound—"No, leave it"—and physically remove his paws from his face. Work quickly, and then begin to move again.

The first walk or two can feel a little complicated. Don't give up on it, though, because the reward is well worth it. So many of my clients can now walk large, strong dogs well (without pulling) for the first time in their lives. Just get past that initial chaotic stage and you will both be happier on the walk. Keep your goal in mind and don't give up.

Don't allow your dog to remove it and give up, or he will win and think he has a choice. It should be your decision to remove it. It will get easier and eventually he'll be able to hang out with it on and leave it alone. It is *not* harmful or painful. In fact, for a pulling dog it is more comfortable than a standard neck collar, which can choke your dog.

Until your dog is used to the head collar, take him out alone if you have other dogs. Later you will be surprised how easily you can walk him and his buddies at the same time.

Leashes

A 6-foot leash is a good length for training and exercise walks. Get one that feels comfortable to your hand. I do not recommend retractable leashes because they don't provide enough control for obedience training.

Later, in advanced training, you'll need a training lead (called a long-line training leash) of about 25 feet (see photo). It is usually made of cotton blend and has a clip that can attach to your dog's collar. It is an excellent

tool when teaching a come command from a distance. Do not use the retractable kind because you don't want your dog to rely on the feeling of being reeled in. You want him to come on his own in preparation for off-leash recall.

Commands

Dogs have the ability to learn a lot of language. When you begin your obedience program, it is important that you save certain command words for when on-leash and for when you are planning on backing up the command if it fails. You want these words to have a lot of meaning to your dog. If you tell him to come while he is off-leash (before he has been off-leash trained) and he doesn't come, you have just severely weakened the meaning of that word for your dog because he knows you cannot catch him. You can of course use these command words off-leash after you have completed the obedience program and your dog is off-leash trained. But when your dog is just learning the words, they have to have a serious meaning for him.

The bottom line is that if you want your dog to listen to your commands, you must very consistently make those commands have meaning. In order for a command to have meaning, you begin to use that word only when your dog is on-leash and you are doing a training session and teaching him at that moment. Use another word to call your dog if you are in the early stages of training and your dog is off-leash but not yet trained well. For example, say something like "Hey, pup" to get your dog to come rather than use the actual word "come." You are saving that word for use only when you have your dog on-leash to back up the word if he doesn't come. That way, whenever he hears the word "come," he knows that that is a serious word and he *always* has to come, with no exceptions.

If you use your command words only when you want to make sure that command is completed, those words will have a lot of meaning to your dog.

Tone of Voice

The sound and tone of your voice can affect the success of commands. In my experience, men often are better at sounding authoritative for commands because of the deepness of their tone, and women naturally are better at offering praise because the tone of their voice is softer. Your command and your praise should sound different. If you are a woman, try to make your voice a little deeper and sharper for commands, similar to how a man would sound. The command should be sharp and fast: "Spot, sit." When you say "sit," it should sound sharp, fast, deep, and authoritative. It should not sound loud or angry, just matter-of-fact with leadership. If you are male, practice praising your dog with a softer, sweeter tone, similar to a female voice. This way the command sounds authoritative and the praise sounds soft.

Because you are asking your dog to do something when giving a command, say his name first to gain his attention (keep the name positive). Here are commands where you use your dog's name before asking the command:

- "Spot, sit"
- "Spot, down"—for lying down, not for jumping on you
- "Spot, stay"
- "Spot, come"
- "Spot, give"—when you want your dog to drop something from his mouth and give it to you
- "Spot, release"—when you are telling your dog it is okay to end his obedience and he can be free until you ask for something again. (This is a very important command because it distinguishes between when he should be serious and listening to your commands and when the lesson has ended. See the section on this command [page 100] for detailed information.)

Do *not* say your dog's name when disciplining or trying to stop a behavior because you don't want him to associate his name with anything negative. Again, do not use loud anger or frustration in your tone. Use your authoritative, deep voice as a leader. Here are commands where you do *not* say your dog's name first:

- "Quiet"—when trying to stop barking
- "Off"—when your dog is jumping on you or to get him off the couch
- "Leave it"—for things you want your dog to leave alone
- "No"—add words to your "no" commands, for example, No bite, No chew, No sniff.

Remember, your dog can learn many words, so keep him challenged by adding more and more. You can name all your dog's toys, balls, bones, etc. When giving your dog the item, make sure you use a name to describe it every time so he can learn it: "Find your chew bone!" "Go get your duck." "Get your ball." "Find your KONG." Have fun with your dog and teach him lots of words!

Your Dog "Forgets" Commands

Dog training is an ongoing process. Your expectations for your dog and the rules he must follow should be a consistent daily part of your life. Many people take their dog to a training class where they practice obedience every day. But when the class ends the dog appears to forget the commands. What really happened is that the dog's guardian stopped practicing and being consistent in the training. For example, if you tell your dog to come but you don't follow through if he comes or not, the command loses its meaning. So the next time you ask him to come, he doesn't. Did he forget, or did he figure out he doesn't really have to come when you call?

Once your dog understands you don't expect him to follow the rules every day, he'll probably stop following them because you aren't being clear. Imagine a teacher who suddenly stops collecting homework. Pretty soon the students won't bother doing it.

★ Clear and Consistent Q & A ★

Q I have a 1-year-old golden retriever, Sunny. She went to puppy school and did pretty well, but the commands we taught (sit, come, down, and leave it) seem to have worn off. How can we solve this problem?

A Dog training is an ongoing, daily task. If you do not keep up with the training that Sunny previously learned, she will "forget" the training. Actually, she didn't really forget—she realized you are not being consistent, so she won't be either!

Keep up with your daily expectations of Sunny in obedience and she should soon be responding well to your commands again.

Proper Positioning

During obedience training, you should have a nice loop in your leash so that your dog does not feel pressure on his neck by having a tight collar (see photo at right).

For teaching let's go, heel, sit, down, and stays, you want your dog at your left side with his right ear parallel to you (see photo below, left). With your dog immediately next to you, you have better control. If you walk in this position, your dog can better see you and go at your pace and also see when you are making turns or stopping.

In the photo below, right, the dog is too far in front of the handler and will not be able to see when she is making a turn. Also, when your dog is too far in front he gets more distracted and harder to control for the obedience exercises. The incorrect position puts the dog in control and often causes him to pull on the leash.

When you begin your obedience, refer to this section and photos for proper positioning of you and your dog.

Sincerity and Timing of Praise

Praise is one of the factors that make dog training successful. But it is important to remember that praise needs to be genuine, not mechanical. Your dog cares less what words you use but more about the energy projection and sincerity of that praise. This becomes so important because when your dog senses that you are truly happy that he performed well, he will begin to look to you to see if he is doing okay. This means that he is focused more on you. That is your main goal in dog training, anyway, getting your dog to actually focus on you.

The sound and tone of your voice can affect the success of both praise and commands. Praise should sound sweet and enthusiastic. Commands should sound authoritative and deep in tone. As mentioned previously, women naturally have a softer voice and men tend to have deep and authoritative tones. Your commands and your praise should sound different from one another. Sincere praise should be natural—you love your dog and he loves you.

Timing of Praise

Diane had a medium-size mixed breed who was very sweet but a handful of muscle and energy. Homer really did want to please and do the right thing; you could just see that about him. During our session I talked with Diane about improving the timing of her praise when Homer performs well because that emphasizes to him exactly what he did that was right. If your timing is off, you will miss the opportunity to tell your dog you like what he did and you want him to do that again, just like that.

The Importance of Sincerity and Timing

Diane began to get the timing right, but she was so focused on the timing that she forgot to feel the *genuine* praise for Homer when he performed a command well. "Good dog" would come out of her mouth at the right time, but it was very flat and mechanical, not at all something that seemed to tell Homer she was happy with him. To Homer, it didn't matter so much what words she used as the feeling behind those words (it's the music, not the lyrics). I encouraged Diane to really *feel* happy and sincerely say the words with an enthusiastic, upbeat tone.

Genuine praise is a payment to your dog for performing well and it lets him know he pleased you. So he wants to repeat the behavior that resulted in the praise.

Being able to praise with the correct timing and sincerity can take practice, but you'll get there. Diane soon was able to coordinate it all and be genuine with Homer while at the same time having good timing. She was on the right track to having a well-behaved dog.

Genuine praise with good timing gets your dog's attention right away and there is a strong bond between the two as you become in sync. From then on, dog training goes well because your dog is looking to you for that pride. You can actually see your dog being happier and having more fun. I am not making this stuff up! It really makes a difference.

> It is important to use a different tone for praise than for the command. If you tell your dog to sit in the same tone you say "Good dog," it doesn't come across that he is getting rewarded for performing well.

Praise and Affection

Try to give praise and affection to your dog only when he is relaxed and when he has done something to please you. If you give affection at the wrong time, you reward bad behavior. I observed a woman at the park the other day with a cute, small dog in her arms, homemade sweater and all. Every time someone passed too close, her dog would start barking and growling. In response, the woman would pet and stroke him, no doubt trying to calm him. In the woman's mind she was trying to calm her dog, but in the dog's mind he was being rewarded for the aggressive behavior.

I've also witnessed shy dogs showing signs of high anxiety and their guardians

> Every time you pet your dog, think about what behavior you are rewarding.

petting them and offering lots of attention in hopes that will make their dogs feel better. In our human world that might seem right, but in the dog world, you are rewarding the shy, anxious behavior and making it worse.

Food Rewards

Food rewards are a very good way to help you gain focus from your dog. You can use any type of food that is healthy for your dog and that your dog loves. Some people use training treats bought from the store, or you can use carrot pieces, frozen peas, or other vegetables your dog likes, or even tiny bits of cooked chicken or meat without bones. Talk with your veterinarian about your dog's diet for what and how much is right for your dog.

Sometimes play is more important to your dog than food, so use a favorite tennis ball, squeaky toy, or whatever object your dog has to have and is willing to work for. When I use the word "treat" throughout the book, it can also mean a toy or your genuine praise if that is what motivates your dog the most.

Always using food treats in training has a downside, though. My client Chris had a beautiful, tall, black Lab who seemed to be very well trained. Whenever Chris asked Jo-Jo to sit, you saw a perfect sit; when asked to go down, you saw a perfect down. What was the problem, you wonder? When Jo-Jo performed these tasks, Chris had a treat in his hand. When Chris didn't have a treat in his hand, Jo-Jo refused to do anything. As far as Jo-Jo was concerned, he'd happily work for food—but only for food.

I am not saying not to use food treats. They are very good for beginning obedience and introducing many situations. But the key is to use them sparingly and randomly. Your goal is that your dog will also perform the command without a treat even being near you. Use the treats for motivation when needed, but also practice without them. Other forms of reward to use are praise, affection, and favorite toys. It can be a good idea to mix up all three of these forms of reward.

★ Treat Q & A ★

Q *I know that a lot of commands can be achieved with the reward of treats or praise. My two dogs (a 5-year-old Lab mix and an 11-month-old Dutch shepherd mix) have learned a lot with the rewards of treats. And it's amazing how fast they learn!*

But what do I do if they become so focused on the treat they pay no heed to the command?

Example: Zak (the young one) has learned from Nitro all about retrieving a tennis ball. The issue is the drop or out command. Nitro has it down pat, treat or no treat. Zak, on the other hand, plays "keep away"; he will not drop or release the ball unless there is a treat involved (and he knows when you're faking!).

Then when he sees I have the "goodie bag," he forgets all about the tennis ball, won't even give it a second look. He is so focused on getting a treat; forget about asking him to retrieve the ball again. Then Nitro gets in on the act because she's afraid she's going to miss out on some goodies, and I get mobbed. Thankfully, they've both learned sit!

There may be times when I won't always have a pocketful of treats.

A Over the years I have seen many dogs who will perform only for treats. Treats are great to use for beginning obedience but should be randomly used as a dog advances in his training.

If you use a treat every time, your dogs become reliant on them. The trick is to use them randomly, so sometimes they get a treat and all the other times they receive hearty, genuine physical praise. Dogs can learn without treats. Good praise should be as good as a treat. Just saying "Good dog" isn't enough. You have to really, deep down inside feel happy that your dog performed well or he won't "feel" your praise. If you are mechanical about the praise, they won't feel rewarded. Always be very genuine in your praise and you'll find you can replace those treats with warm, wonderful praise.

In your situation, Zak is so focused on treats that he loses focus on the task. I would say get rid of the treats. Don't even bring them with you.

Definitely do not allow Zak to play keep away, though. If he doesn't drop the ball on the return of fetch, the game ends, and that is not fun. Don't go and try to get the ball from your dog, just wait. If he doesn't drop the ball, you don't play with him. This works for most dogs. Maybe Zak doesn't love fetch so he doesn't care if the game ends. You might need another motivator, such as an exchange. Offer another ball or favorite toy he loves so he has to drop the ball to receive the new item. Dogs are very smart. Eventually Zak will understand that if he wants to play fetch with you, he has to drop the ball.

4

STEP TWO—TRAINING BEGINS

If you think dogs can't count, try putting three dog biscuits in your
pocket and then giving Fido only two of them.
~Phil Pastoret~

Reading Dogs' Body Language

The most important thing in communication is to
hear what isn't being said.
~Peter Drucker~

When your dog is calm, notice his body language. Observe how relaxed his ears, face, and tail are. His mouth may be slightly open. But when something gets your dog's attention, notice how he changes. His mouth generally closes, his ears go forward to listen, and his body looks tenser.

You can learn a lot at a dog park observing dogs. For example, if a dog's tail

- is low and tucked, the dog is insecure or submissive.
- wags sideways quickly with a wide sweep, generally the dog is friendly.
- slowly wags side to side or up and down, the dog is uncertain.

A good greeting between dogs occurs in an arc, not a straight line face-to-face. They move to smell each other in the area to the side of their mouth and their genitals. According to the AKC, your dog's sense of smell is thought to be 100,000 times stronger than yours. Dogs have scent glands on different parts of their body. These scents send all kinds of messages to other dogs, including the dog's gender and if he is intact. Dogs generally do not make direct eye contact during a good greeting.

Sometimes dogs try to make themselves look taller by stiffening and straightening their legs during a greeting. This is fine if the dogs move onto something else, or it can be the beginning of threatening behavior. A dog crouching, while holding his head low, ears pinned back, tail tucked between his legs, in a more submissive position (his hair may be standing up on his back and his teeth are slightly showing) is exhibiting signs of fear. The fearful dog's response may be to lunge aggressively or to run away.

Pay attention to a dog who acts dominant. He stands tall over another dog, generally with his tail straight up, his hair may be standing on his back, and he looks directly at the other dog with his teeth showing. If the other dog decides to submit to this dominant dog, he may lie down and roll over on his back and not look at the other dog.

How you handle situations with your dog can affect his response. If you are nervous or showing anxiety, your dog is likely to pick up on that, and this can lead to trouble. Stay calm when your dog is greeting another dog. If you notice threatening behavior, remove your dog from the situation and continue on. A good leader learns to read her dog's body language so she can act *before* it's too late.

Your dog feels your body's energy and he reads your body language. If you are fearful, unsure, or angry, he knows it. The energy you project to him will affect his behavior. If you want your dog to get off the couch and he refuses, but deep inside you know you will let him stay if he protests enough, he knows that too. Go into each situation knowing inside yourself that you are leader and that you decide what to do and what not to do. He will instantly sense this and do what you want.

Some clients report that when they are doing obedience with their dogs and I am nearby, their dogs listen to them, but when I go home they don't respond as well. What is really happening is that when I am there, the guardians feel more confident and the dogs observe that confidence and feel the leadership, and they listen better! Once the guardians can capture that same feeling of calm, clear, consistent, leadership when I am not there, their dogs listen better.

Never display anger toward your dog. He will know it and see you as a weak, unhinged leader, and this will make him not trust you or listen to you. You may even cause fear, and that may trigger aggression.

Never hit your dog. Not only is this extremely cruel, but you are also giving a signal for your dog to fear you, which will have a negative impact on his behavior, causing you more problems down the line. Good dog training does not involve physical harm to your dog. Always take a break if you feel you are losing control. Remember your dog does not intentionally do things to upset you, he just hasn't been trained otherwise or has not had his needs properly met.

Dogs communicate through their senses and observations of body language, not so much through verbal language. You can talk all you want to your dog, but he is reading your body language, not listening to your words. This is why it is vitally important to *feel* calm and confident when working with your dog. He will know if you are agitated, angry, or upset, and it will make him agitated, worried, or confused. He will also know when you are not feeling confident and sure of yourself as a leader.

After understanding your dog's mind, you can move on to teaching obedience. Here's how.

1. Build your foundation first. Introduce the commands, and when you are sure Rover understands, add small distractions to ensure comprehension. You'll see that a stay without a distraction is different from staying while distracted.
2. Repeat, repeat, repeat. Dogs learn through performing their commands successfully over and over in all types of situations.
3. Initially, it is *very* important to use command words (come, stay, etc.) only when you are training on-leash. If you tell Rover to come and he gets away with not coming, you can undo the meaning of the command and Rover will not learn to come consistently. You will eventually have off-leash command ability, but that comes later, after lots of practice on-leash.
4. Once you ask Rover to perform a command, make sure that he actually does it. If you tell him to sit and he doesn't, and you just let it go, he won't ever know when he has to perform the command and when he doesn't. But if *every* time you say sit he *has* to sit, then he's likely to sit every time you ask.
5. Consistency and good technique with lots of practice get the fastest results. Once you decide to teach or change a behavior, you must be consistent with that decision every time. For example, if you allow Rover to jump on you sometimes but don't want him to jump when you are dressed nicely, he won't understand. He doesn't know or care about clothes. Your training must be very clear, because dogs don't read between the lines like humans do.

Starting Your Obedience Program

Today you begin a new life with your dog! Now that you understand more about your dog, you are better equipped to begin the training program.

A Quiet Environment

The first form of training is teaching your dog to perform commands in your quiet home environment so he can fully focus on you and truly understand what you are asking him to do. You may think your dog knows the word "sit" because he performs the sit sometimes, but if your dog is in an environment with a lot of distractions, he may not perform the sit. This means he doesn't *fully* understand that when you ask him to sit, he must do it.

Don't be surprised if your dog performs better at home than outside. At home there isn't anything better for him to see or sniff. But outside, the dog across the street is more interesting than you. At home he's already had a chance to sniff and check out everything, and maybe you are interesting to him in that environment, but not where there are new things to smell and discover!

How can you get your dog to listen *outside* too? Asking him to perform a command while he is strongly focused on something way more exciting than you often fails if you are too close to the object of distraction too early in your training. It's like taking a test when you haven't studied the material or prepared yourself. I'll teach you the material so you can train your dog to be prepared, and then you'll have success.

Assuming your dog or puppy is learning these commands for the first time, start at the beginning. Your dog may understand some commands well, but not others, so it can be beneficial for you to read from this point anyway.

Rewards

Food treats and favorite toys are a wonderful way to get your dog to focus on you and be rewarded for doing well. In the initial part of this type of training I usually use treats. They are a great tool for teaching your dog to associate the commands with a positive reward, and also makes him focus more on you. Later use treats only occasionally because you do not want your dog to perform a command only because you have a treat. You want him to learn to perform the command without the treat.

Consider your dog's diet when deciding on the treat to use and try some to see what he likes best. The treat should be something your dog absolutely loves and has to have. Be sure that when you are giving your dog treats, you do not overfeed him. Adjust his regular food intake if needed so that he does not gain weight. Do not overdo the amount of treats and keep the pieces small. There are special pouches you can buy that you fill with treats and clip to your pants, or just be creative with how you want to keep the treats easily accessible to you so your timing is good.

Summary for Success

Success is where preparation and opportunity meet.
~Bobby Unser~

REASONS TO TEACH OBEDIENCE (SIT, DOWN, STAY, HEEL, COME)
- Your dog learns that you are the leader. Your dog needs and *wants* to have a leader and to understand his role in the family. Without a clear leader, your dog may take on that leader role himself, causing behavioral issues such as aggression, separation anxiety, and fear.
- You can change undesirable behavior, including jumping, excessive barking, etc.
- Your dog learns desirable behavior, like a controlled sit, down, stay, come when called, and walks without pulling.
- Your dog is easier to be around and take out in all situations.

DAILY ROUTINE FOR A WELL-ADJUSTED, OBEDIENT, HAPPY DOG
- Maintain obedience through daily practice.
- Be the leader and enforce your house rules, such as when to wake up, when to eat, where to go, at what pace to walk and stop to rest, etc. If your dog is making these decisions, you are not being the leader.
- Consistently keep the rules clear, for example, your dog should stop barking when you ask him to, no jumping on you, no possessiveness of toys, no aggressiveness toward other dogs or people. Remember, *you* own the house and *you* make the rules.
- Exercise! Take your dog for walks twice a day for *at least* 30 minutes each (longer is better). Practice obedience along the way.
- Feed your dog calmly. Ask him to sit and stay while you place the food down, then release him to eat. Do not set down the food bowl if your dog is jumping on you or barking; wait until he is calm.
- Don't allow your dog to beg for food at your mealtime. You decide where he should lie at mealtime and stick to it.

- Leave the house only when you have met *all* of your dog's needs and you and your dog are both calm.
- If your dog is experiencing separation anxiety, do not make a big deal about coming and going, and pet him only when he gets into a relaxed state. Do not make eye contact, talk to, or pet your dog before leaving or when returning until he is calm. (See the behavioral modification section, page 140, for more info.)
- You decide where your dog sleeps and make it clear to him.
- Every human in the house must be a calm, clear, consistent leader and enforce the same rules.
- Give praise and attention when your dog is relaxed, when he has changed an unwanted behavior into something you asked for, or after he has responded well to a rule or command. Do not pet your dog when he is jumping on you, barking, being fearful, possessive, dominant, aggressive, or breaking any of your clear rules. When you give affection, you reinforce the behavior that happened just prior to it.

Release Command

Teach this command early in your training.

This command gives your dog a clear indication of when he can release himself from a command and is free to do what he wants. For example, say your dog is in a stay and you have decided he can break that stay or you are walking in a controlled way and you've decided he can be free to go pee on a certain tree, use the release command. He is basically allowed to do what he wants in this command except pull or drag you by the leash somewhere—that is never allowed.

I used to use the word "okay" as the release word, but we use that word so much in our daily conversations that it is confusing to dogs. Some people use "free." I prefer "release," but it doesn't matter what word you use as long as it is your word for releasing your dog and you use the same word every time.

This command is very important for your dog to learn because it makes the time you are training serious and focused. He knows he is on duty, so to speak, until released.

To teach this, I use an upward motion where I raise both my hands to the sky as I say "release" in a very positive tone (see photo at right). Ideally, you want him to run to you for affection after being released, rather then bolt away from you.

Give your dog physical praise and attention at the time of the release if you have just completed a session. It is important to release him when he has been performing well; you want all training sessions to end on a positive note because that is what he will remember.

If your dog starts to pull you to a tree and then you decide to release him after he's pulled you, he got what he wanted and was not behaving in an obedient way. And how can he tell when to focus if he gets to release *himself* whenever he pulls hard enough? You want him to go to the tree only *after* he's been released.

The release command is a lot of fun for you and your dog, and is an extra bit of reward. Watch your dog perform an obedience task well, receive praise, then get released. He will be truly happy and you have just taught him something really well!

The Let's Go No-Pull Walk

The let's go command is a good way to start to teach your dog not to pull on walks but instead to walk at your side. For the purposes of this lesson I will speak as though your dog is on your left side.

Your dog's right ear should be parallel to your left leg (see photo on next page). If he is farther ahead of you, he cannot physically see when you make a turn. When you are beginning this exercise, do a lot of figure eight turns. Do not walk a long distance with your dog without making many quick turns first. This is of course what will happen initially,

but as your dog catches on, you will be able to walk farther without the turns.

If you want to just have an exercise walk, I recommend using the head collar or body harness (see pages 83–84). The early stages of teaching the let's go command require a lot of turns; it is not meant for your long exercise walk at this point.

Start the training exercise without any distractions so your dog can concentrate on you.

1. Put your dog's regular neck collar on with attached leash. With your dog to your left, you should have a nice loop in the leash.
2. Start out by saying "Let's go" and immediately offering a treat.
3. Say "Let's go" again and offer the treat after a couple seconds. Repeat, this time waiting 4 seconds before giving the treat; repeat and wait 6 seconds to give the treat. You are slowly building the time your dog is waiting for the treat so he learns to look at you and focus on you.
4. Now say "Let's go" and start to walk, then treat right away after just a couple of steps.
5. Keep increasing the length of time between saying "Let's go" and walking a few additional steps, before treating again.
6. Once you get the hang of it, start thinking about the position your dog is in. If your dog walks in front of you, then you don't treat. Get him to walk next to you when you treat. Wherever you treat is the place he thinks he is supposed to be.
7. Don't expect too much too soon. Practice just a little bit at a time when you are feeling calm and patient.
8. End each session positively.
9. Don't treat your dog if he is jumping on you. Remember, he'll repeat the behavior he was just treated for.
10. Keep increasing the period of time between walking and treating.

Now you can add turns.

1. Offer a food lure during your turn while you say "Let's go" and start walking into your turn (see photo at right). This makes the turn positive and puts your dog's focus on you.
2. If your dog starts to pull ahead of you at any time, stop dead in your tracks. Do not take one step farther or say anything to your dog.
3. When your dog looks back at you wondering why you aren't moving, praise him, loosen the leash, and walk again.
4. Repeat every time your dog pulls.

This process teaches your dog that a loose leash means you are happy and he gets to walk, and pulling on the leash means he doesn't get to go anywhere. For this to work, you cannot *ever* give in to the pulling. Don't expect to get very far when you first start out with this, but over time, with consistent practice, your dog will understand not to pull.

Over a period of a few weeks of daily practice, you and your dog should get really good at this and walk much farther with your dog at your side, not pulling. Now think about offering treats alternately with genuine praise so that your dog can perform a nice let's go with or without treats.

After your dog is focused on you and doing the turns well, turn without a food lure but still using the let's go command.

It is best to do your turns quickly so you surprise your dog. The idea is that he won't know where you will turn so he has to pay attention to you. Remember to have a nice small loop in your leash so there is no pressure on your dog's neck.

Whenever you begin to walk or make a turn, repeat "let's go." When your dog is in the proper position, praise him. Your praise must be genuine and given at the exact moment your dog is in the correct position. Make it very clear at which point you are happy with him.

Your dog should not be sniffing the ground or pulling during a let's go walk. He should be focused on you and where you are going and how fast your pace is. Your dog can enjoy this type of serious walk, and it is good for him because he will like the mental challenge.

> To teach the let's go walk well, change your pace and turn often, so that your dog is always paying attention to you.

Practice this daily. When you both get very good at it, move on to teaching a good heel (page 131), which is more formal and with higher expectations.

★ Listening on Walks Q & A ★

Q *Our family recently acquired two dogs quite suddenly. One is a springer spaniel (Prince) a family member got, then decided she didn't want after a year of ownership and lack of training. She rescued Prince when he was roughly 2 years old, so I think he is about 3–4 years old now. The other is a dalmatian (Ruby) we rescued. She is 2 years old. She is sweet and loving, but you can tell that her previous owners didn't want to take the time to train her or give her love.*

I haven't owned dogs since I was a little girl so I feel quite lost. Both dogs seem to understand simple commands like stay and down. Getting them to obey consistently is another story. Taking them on walks is somewhat frustrating. They are powerful and it's hard to control them. When we walk them, we stop them often and make them sit patiently (or as patiently as they can), then start the walk again.

Prince acts as though we don't exist when he is off the leash, though. It's like he loses all ability to hear, see, or obey us, and will take off running. A few weeks ago he wiggled out of his collar while on a walk and took off and we couldn't do anything to get him to come back. We chased him for a long time but he was simply too fast and was gone. We ended up picking him up at the pound the next day (for almost $150).

Ruby seems eager to please us, but she gets so excited and has a hard time sitting still long enough for us to teach her basic obedience. When she is in a calm state she seems more willing to listen, make eye contact, and obey.

How do I get Prince to listen consistently even when off a leash? And how do I get Ruby to calm down long enough to listen? I see that you mention the Gentle Leader for walks, but if Prince can slip out of his collar easily, will he also be able to slip out of the Leader?

I am committed to keeping and loving these dogs for a lifetime. They both have such gentle hearts and I couldn't bear them being sent to yet another home. I just need some training so I can train them.

A It is common for dogs who haven't been trained to "act like you don't exist" off-leash. They actually aren't doing anything wrong in their mind because you haven't "trained" them otherwise. In order to be successful off-leash, begin to teach the come while on-leash so that you can back up the command with good timing. Imagine you called Prince to come to you while off-leash and he didn't come: You have now begun to ruin that word for him because he realizes he really doesn't have to come to you. But if Prince was on-leash when you called, you could have made sure he came to you, which makes the command itself have meaning. Of course you will later have that off-leash control, but if you do not first practice it on-leash you cannot have the proper timing to make it extremely successful. Use treats and praise for positive reinforcement. Good off-leash control can take months of daily practice.

Because you are having trouble getting Ruby calm enough to listen to obedience, I recommend that you exercise her *before* the obedience practice. Some dogs need this. Think of it like a little kid who has tons of pent-up energy and you are forcing her to sit still and concentrate on work—that's why schools invented recess! Drain her unreleased energy and she'll be able to concentrate better. She'll be more relaxed and happier too. I highly recommend the Gentle Leader collar, and if you attach it appropriately it should not slip off. A head collar will help prevent Prince's pulling and give you instant control over him.

★ Dog Stalling on Walks Q & A ★

Q *We recently bought an almost 3-year-old Portuguese water dog, named Dreamer. She is wonderful. Our problem is that she has decided not to walk around our neighborhood. We contacted a local trainer and had a lesson. After the lesson I thought about Dreamer and don't feel the methods and the dog match. The dog seems smarter than the method! She is perfect in the house, and when we first got her (about 6 weeks ago) she would go on a walk. About 3 weeks ago she stopped walking. She will go about 12 feet from the door and then stop and sit. I can take her to an off-leash dog park and she behaves beautifully—come, sit, etc. It is like something on a walk reminds her of something she would like to forget. She came from a breeder, and I think that she washed out as a show dog. I managed to get her going a little by carrying her a ways, then we would move on. She is now too smart for that, and I don't need that much of an upper-body workout. The walking problem isn't good for the dog or us.*

A You can change this behavior, because dogs don't really hold on to old memories when you replace them with new experiences. Once you start associating the walk with something positive she'll forget whatever made her stop in the first place.

Try putting Dreamer on a long line (25-foot or more training lead) and just casually walk ahead of her. Turn around and excitedly tempt her to come to you for a delicious treat. When she gets to you, treat her. Then walk ahead and do it again, just as excited. Repeat until she just starts walking, then casually pick up the leash without her even knowing and without *any* pressure on her neck and start walking, offering treats along the way for good behavior.

It is very important that you do not feel sorry for Dreamer or have any kind of stress about it. Your stress or hesitation will affect her and may prevent her from moving past it all. From this moment on you should act as if there is no problem and don't give her any indication that you feel stressed, anxious, or worried. It is hard, because it is human nature to react, but try your best. Take a deep breath and think positive thoughts and send her only positive signals. It is possible that you experienced some kind of stress or discomfort on a walk and that caused Dreamer to react without you even realizing it. But once you become successful moving on that walk, it should all be behind you.

Sit Command

Using a treat to teach your dog to sit is a great positive reinforcement technique for beginning obedience. The act of sitting becomes associated with the command word "sit," and praise or treats create the positive desire to do it.

Positive Reinforcement

Put your dog's regular neck collar on with attached leash. You can use a treat to lure your dog into a sit by placing the treat over your dog's head and moving it up and over the back of his head so that he follows the lure and sits on his own. He then can receive the treat when he completes the sit (see photos below). Repeat and start to use the command just before you use the food lure.

1. Say your dog's name and then say the command "sit."
2. Lure your dog into a sit using the treat.
3. Give the treat as soon as he sits.
4. Repeat.
5. When your dog performs well, start to wean off the treats and offer your praise instead.

If your dog tends to jump up to try to get the food, do not lift your hand upward. Instead, move your hand slowly back, which should encourage your dog to tilt his head back and cause the sit.

Give the treat the instant your dog's rear hits the ground. Don't expect him to stay in a sit at this point. That comes later when you teach the sit-stay command.

THINGS TO REMEMBER ABOUT THE SIT COMMAND
1. Be positive and upbeat in your tone.
2. Say your dog's name and command only once.
3. Treat or praise as soon as your dog completes the command.

As with all new commands, your dog needs a lot of repetition to get really good. Perform this command without any distractions until your dog sits on his own every time you ask.

When your dog starts to really understand the command, you can give a hand signal. Some people like to hold up one finger while they say, "Spot, sit." You can later use the hand signal alone to create the action from a distance.

As with everything dog-related, be consistent. Make sure your dog sits if you ask him to. If he doesn't sit, try physically placing him into a sit by applying pressure at the hips. I've seen people tell their dogs to sit over and over, and when the dogs don't, the guardians just give up. Your dog needs to know that *every time* he hears his name and the command sit, he *has* to do it. So don't ask him to sit unless you have the energy and ability to back it up and make it happen. For easy, daily practice, have your dog sit before offering his food.

Down Command

Teaching your dog to go into a down position is very important. It is a good position for keeping your dog under control and is comfortable for long stays.

Teaching down-stay is wonderful for many reasons. Your dog can greet small children while under control and can wait patiently for you to perform an activity that requires his control.

Begin this command only after you have taught a good sit. Make sure there are no distractions in the early stages of training. You will of course be training your dog with distractions later, as you advance your training.

1. To begin, tell your dog to sit and praise him when he does.
2. Hold a treat below his head with your hand resting on the ground, so that you are luring him to reach down to get the treat. Do not give the treat until he lies

down. Then instantly open your hand and give the treat. If your dog's rear end pops up to get the treat, you may be holding the treat too far ahead. Keep it near his front paws, resting your hand on the ground below him.

3. Keep practicing. Once your dog starts to understand he needs to lie down to receive the treat, start using the verbal command following his name: "Spot, down."

4. Once your dog is responding to the verbal cue to go down, you are ready to begin the more formal command.

Start with your dog in a sit at your left side. Put your dog's regular neck collar on with attached leash (you should be using a regular 6-foot leash). Say your dog's name, then ask the command: "down." While asking him to go down, you can use a hand signal. Your hand is flat, palm facing the ground, at hip level; bring your hand down to the ground (see photo below, left).

The goal is to physically get your dog to lie down, and to praise or treat him immediately once he is down (see photo below, right).

When your dog is consistently doing the command well, start weaning him off the food treats and offering your genuine praise instead. Practice this often. Remember to say his name, then the command, cause the action, then praise.

When your dog confidently goes into a down position every time, you can begin to add distractions in the environment to challenge him and improve his ability over time.

Stay Command

In my opinion, stay is a very a formal command that should be taught consistently and seriously. Enforce to your dog that stay means he does not move out of position. Don't allow him to roll over or stretch to try to reach a smell, or chew grass or anything of the sort. He can shift slightly for more comfort but not stand up or get out of position to do it.

To teach a good stay, you must first have mastered good sit and down commands. You can practice both the sit-stay and the down-stay. If you plan to have your dog in a stay for several minutes or more, a down-stay is more comfortable.

> This note is a great example of how my stay command techniques helped someone:
>
> *"Julie, I am impressed by your insight, especially about stay. I now understand why none of my previous animals ever truly understood this command."*
> *~Kristen from South Carolina.~*

Be sure to exercise your dog well before you ask him to maintain a stay for several minutes. It isn't fair to expect your dog not to move out of a stay if he is full of energy, plus it is a lot harder for you to train him.

Put your dog's regular neck collar on with attached leash. With your dog in a down position, place your hand in front of his face (not touching) and say your dog's name, then the command: "Spot, stay" (see photo on opposite page). At the early stages of teaching a stay, you should squat next to your dog with all focus on him. There should be no distractions at this point.

The secret to teaching a good stay is to catch your dog before he has the chance to stand all the way up. Watch your dog's body language here closely. If you see he is focused on something and his body is tense, it is likely he will try to pop up.

I like to practice the down-stay before the sit-stay because it takes a little longer for a dog to stand up from a down than a sit. When a dog is in a sit-stay position he can pop up really fast. First practice the down-stay and then introduce the sit-stay.

You are trying to get a good stay for only a couple of minutes initially. If your dog pops up, quickly say "No, stay!" in a commanding tone—not angry or frustrated—and put him back into the stay. Ideally, you caught him before he stood up all the way.

While your dog is mastering the stay, you can praise him in a happy tone: "Good stay." If your dog reaches out to find a smell or roll over, stop him and repeat the stay.

Do not stand up or walk a couple steps away yet; it is too early and your timing will not be good. At this point you should not even know what is going on around you because you are so focused on your dog. Do not look around for distractions. Keep your eyes on your dog or you will not be fast enough to catch the break of the stay.

Learn how your dog looks just before he breaks the stay, and then your timing will be really good to stop him. In most dogs, you can see their muscles begin to tighten split seconds before they pop up.

You'll achieve the best stay by not trying to advance before your dog is ready. Don't stand until your dog has been holding the stay for a couple of minutes.

Ending the Stay

Do not let your dog prematurely break the stay. Say you were just about to release him, but he beat you to it and popped up on his own: If you let him get away with this, even though you feel done, you will ruin the command. End all stay sessions with the release command.

STEPS FOR PRACTICING STAY

1. Put your dog into the down position and praise him.
2. Say, "Spot, stay," and praise him in a genuine, happy tone.
3. If your dog pops up, catch the collar quickly with one hand, and place the other hand on his back and say "No, stay" (firmly, without anger) and put him back in the stay. Praise him for the stay.
4. After a few seconds, give your dog the release command and praise him enthusiastically.

5. Repeat.
6. Practice this for a couple of minutes every day, until your dog can gradually increase the amount of time he can stay without popping up.
7. Use good timing to catch your dog from breaking the stay and praise him when he is doing well.

You can advance when your dog can remain in a stay for a couple of minutes without breaking it. To advance, you add small distractions while still squatting next to your dog. Don't stand until your dog has mastered the stay and has not been trying to jump up.

Slowly add more and more distractions and more and more time to the stay. Eventually you can stand up next to your dog when you feel he will not break the stay.

Later you can move to the end of your leash and after that to the end of the 25-foot line.

Read your dog and move slowly to advance. Practice daily for several weeks to be able to leave your squatting position and stand up next to your dog. This may sound like a long time, but if you master this early stage your dog will fully understand the command, and the advancement will go more quickly.

If you stand up and move away from your dog too early and he breaks the stay, your dog will not advance quickly. Believe me, you will be happy you took the time in this early stage to teach him well because a good stay is important out in the dog-human world.

Here's a great example of improper timing leading to failure. Cindy came to me totally frustrated because she had been trying to train her standard poodle, Jasper, to stay, and it wasn't working. I asked her to show me how she was doing it. She placed Jasper in a down, asked him to stay, and then walked away a few steps. Jasper broke the stay. Cindy told him no, then put him back in the stay, repeated the command, and walked away a few steps. Once again, Jasper broke the stay. This is a common way many people try to train their dogs to stay.

So what went wrong? Jasper was fully getting up from the stay, and a precious second or two would pass before Cindy told him "no." This was just enough time to totally be confused. In Jasper's mind, he was getting told no when he already had his mind on something else—perhaps a smell he was investigating or even possibly coming toward Cindy. In his mind he was getting told no for going toward the smell or Cindy, not no for breaking the stay. That second or two doesn't seem like much time to us, but it is just enough time for your dog to move on to something else.

Because Jasper did not understand that he was being told no for breaking the stay, he hadn't learned how to stay. Cindy redid the obedience, staying close to Jasper so she could catch the break in the stay immediately. Jasper quickly began to understand the command. Once Cindy made a small adjustment to the way she was doing it, Jasper understood. He eventually got so good at stays that Cindy even practiced them on her trail walks and proudly watched as Jasper maintained the stay while other hikers and dogs passed by.

Practice the sit-stay every time you feed your dog. Tell him to sit and praise him. Then tell him to stay. Wait a few seconds and then release him to eat. Gradually you should be able to put the food bowl down and make your dog maintain a sit-stay before releasing him to eat. This is one area where the release command comes in very handy. You decide when to break the stay. If your dog breaks the stay and eats the food without you releasing him, you will ruin the command for them.

Imagine bringing your dog to your local café with outdoor seating and having him lie quietly next to you while you enjoy your food and drink. Or imagine that a small child wants to pet your dog and you can put him in a nice down-stay so she can safely pet him. Or perhaps you have a guest who is afraid of dogs. You can put your dog in a down-stay without concern while you greet your guest. There are so many benefits to having a nice down-stay with your dog.

Come (Recall) Command

Teaching a good come command (also called a recall) is very important for many reasons. For one, you can have your dog off-leash and feel confident about getting him back to you at any time. But it takes a lot of practice, as does all of the obedience, before it is successful off-leash.

A great way to start getting your dog to want to come to you is to play hide-and-seek with him. Hide somewhere in the house and make a silly noise to have your dog find you. When he gets to you, offer lots of enthusiastic praise or even a treat. This sets up bonding with your dog and he starts to get the idea that it is really fun to get to you.

You can also have someone hold on to your dog, saying "Find him" or "Where is she?" or whatever words you want to give while you go hide in another room. Sometimes being held back a bit makes your dog want to get to you even more. You can practice this at friends' homes too. Your dog will soon learn it is a lot of fun to come to you; then it will be time to move on to a more formal command.

In order to later be successful off-leash, begin to teach the come while on-leash so that you can back up the command with good timing. Suppose you have called your dog to come to you while off-leash and he doesn't come. You have now begun to ruin that word for him because he realizes he really doesn't have to come to you. But if your dog is on-leash when you call him, you can make sure he comes to you no matter what, which makes the command have more meaning. Of course, you will later have that off-leash control, but first your dog has to practice it on-leash.

Teaching the Come Command

1. Put your dog's leash and neck collar on and get a treat ready in your hand.
2. Walk to the end of the leash (see photo below), show the treat to your dog, and very enthusiastically say his name and the command: "Spot, come!"
3. Give treat.

The photo below shows the dog in a sit, but he can be doing anything he wants when you practice this command. When you begin this exercise, your dog is in a release mode doing whatever he wants before you call him. If he comes to you before you call him, that's great too! Eventually your dog may start coming to you before you call, and that is a good thing. Dogs are smart and often begin to anticipate your moves.

Always say your dog's name first to gain attention. Sound very encouraging with this command because you want it exciting and wonderful for your dog to get to you. When

your dog gets to you, reward him instantly with the treat. He should gobble it down and have a lot of focus on you now.

Getting to you must be better than the smell or sight of another exciting experience that your dog might be focused on, so you have to make it like a party when he does get to you. You can also offer praise with petting or a favorite toy as a reward for getting to you. Make sure there are no distractions and you are acting very inviting right now (like squatting with a treat) when you begin to teach this command. If your dog still does not come to you, try walking away to get him to follow.

Do not say "come" over and over. Saying it once after your dog's name is enough. (Sometimes you can repeat the command a little more in the early stages, but when you begin to advance, only say it once.) You do not want your dog to get into the habit of waiting until the sixth time you've said it!

When you are showing your dog the treat, hold your hand the same way every time. Later, when you are not using treats, you will hold your hand in the same way as you held a treat. You're giving a visual cue along with the command. Later your dog will remember that treat and reward when he sees your hand in the same position. He will focus on you more when you begin to use treats less.

How close should your dog be when he receives the treat? Close enough that you could reach out and grab his collar if needed. You want to make clear to your dog that "Come" means come to *you,* not several feet away and then bolt. Some dogs who are praised on their way to coming think that's good enough and do not get all the way to their handlers. Make sure you praise when he reaches you.

Do not give the treat until your dog actually reaches you. But do treat *immediately* when he reaches you (don't delay it so that he's not clear what you are happy about).

Some people like to make their dogs sit when they come. My preference is to first praise for the come and then later add the sit when your dog is doing well. Expecting a dog to sit when he comes isn't necessary unless you are having problems with your dog taking off the second he reaches you (so you cannot even get hold of him if you need to). Increase your enthusiasm for your dog reaching you.

If your dog does not come to you at this point it is usually for one of three reasons: (1) your treat or praise is not enticing enough; (2) something is distracting your dog; or (3) at some point in the past you (probably unintentionally) made it a negative experience for your dog to get to you. Go to a quiet environment with a treat and be *very* positive and excited when your dog gets to you!

I had a client whose dog was fearful of coming. One time she disciplined the dog when he came, because she was angry that the dog peed on the carpet. She called the dog to her to show her anger. But that actually disciplined the dog for coming to her, not for peeing. The dog thought he did something wrong for coming. Never make the mistake of indicating that your dog is wrong for coming to you. Not only will your dog stop trusting you, he will not want to come to you either! Always encourage your dog to come to you and make it very positive when he does. This instills in him that coming to you is a very happy thing that he will always want to do.

Practice this several times a day for several days or a few weeks in different parts of your home. Your goal here is to be successful 100 percent of the time with the recall, and for your dog to think it is just one big fun game. You will, of course, be making it a little harder later, but it will still be positive.

If your dog is off-leash and doesn't come to you, do not chase him—he may think it is a keep-away game. Instead, run in the opposite direction making a loud, silly noise while waving your arms. This will entice him to come to you! A friend of mine had just gotten a new dog. He got loose because the children had opened the door, and out he went! The kids ran out to catch him, but he was too fast and was getting farther away from the house. I instructed everyone to run back to the house, making their loud, silly noises, and guess what? The dog ran after them and back into the house!

ANGER

Do not get angry at your dog for housebreaking accidents or any other unwanted behavior. Anger sends the message to your dog that you are a weak leader and not trustworthy—and he won't listen to you. If you feel angry, take a time-out and do not interact with your dog then. To prevent housebreaking accidents, you must catch your dog in the act. Calmly and firmly say "No" and take him outside to eliminate. Never discipline your dog after an accident has already occurred; it is too late. See the housetraining section (page 44) for more information on this topic.

Leave It Command

Use the leave it command to keep your dog away from anything you do not want him to touch, smell, or investigate.

1. Get delicious treats ready. Put a treat in your fist while your dog is watching. Have another treat in your other hand, hidden behind your back that your dog doesn't know about.

2. Show the hand with the treat and say, "Leave it" in an authoritative way. He may smell it and begin to try to lick at your hand, so repeat the command if necessary. Watch closely: The second he stops licking or sniffing and leaves your hand alone, quickly give the treat from your hidden hand by tossing it on the ground in front of him. The second he stops *trying* to get it is the second he gets a surprise treat on the ground.

3. Most dogs learn very quickly to leave it while they wait for the other treat. They are learning that when they leave it, they get rewarded.

4. Over time you can place the object or treat you want him to leave alone somewhere openly on the ground. As soon as you toss it down, tell your dog to "Leave it" in your leadership tone. Then, the second you notice he didn't go for it, offer a treat he can have. Gradually, over a period of weeks, you can extend the amount of time you expect him to leave it before you give a treat.

5. You can also begin to transfer the leave it to anything you don't want your dog to smell or eat, such as garbage on the street. If you are passing garbage, practice the command. When he is able to pass by the garbage without going for it, make sure you praise or treat the second he passes it.

6. You can also use this command to separate what your dog is allowed to have in the house and what he is not, for example, your children's toys (or your shoes, or people food). Toss a child's toy on the floor and say "Leave it." When he leaves it alone, throw his own toy to him.

7. If you want your dog to stop chasing the cat or squirrels, for example, you can also use the command.

8. If you use the command consistently and back up your dog's success with praise or treats, he will soon understand.

Go Back Command

Your dog is standing over a toy he wants you to throw for him. The second you reach down to pick it up, he beats you to it and may even accidentally take a nip out of your hand. This can be a dangerous situation, especially for children. It's an excellent opportunity to begin teaching your dog the go back command, which will make him take a few steps back whenever you ask him to.

Hold a treat in your hand and walk into your dog's space while at the same time gesturing for him to go back. Block him so his only option is to take steps backward. When he steps back, give the treat. Repeat until your dog just goes back with your arm gesturing and your command "Go back."

If your dog is constantly underfoot when you are trying to feed him, tell him to go back. When he does go back, put down the food bowl. If your dog likes to play fetch and drops the ball at your feet, tell him to go back and throw the ball as soon as he does. Food and toys are both great ways to reinforce new commands.

How Often Should I Practice Obedience?

Great things are done by a series of
small things brought together.
~Vincent van Gogh~

I suggest you do several 5- to 10-minute obedience sessions every day. This is not a hard-and-fast rule, though. If you and your dog feel like doing a half-hour session or longer, go for it! It is also a great idea to get into the habit of asking your dog to perform a command immediately before he gets fed. That way, you automatically do two short sessions every day and he gets rewarded with food. Get the food ready and tell him to come, or have him sit before you give the food. You can have your dog sit before he goes outside, or lie down to receive a bone. If you make a habit of doing something the same way every day, that becomes a part of your routine too so you'll end up with more practice time. Also try doing obedience everywhere you go, even if only for a few minutes. Practice obedience on walks, at parks, at friends' houses, etc.

Always end each session positively after your dog has done something well and you have released him. The most important rule is to have the right state of mind when doing obedience.

Never practice obedience when you feel tired or frustrated or angry. You need to feel calm and confident and secure in what you are asking your dog to do. Along with the formal sessions, you should be a calm leader all the time, every day at home. Your house rules should always be followed. When you are consistent with the rules, your dog will learn them quickly.

When you expect your dog to follow rules of the home, he will also be better at obedience overall. His leader is asking something of him, and he will trust you more if you've been consistent.

Inconsistency on your part with any rules results in a dog who is inconsistent in obeying your commands. Your dog doesn't want to be confused all the time, never sure what behavior earns a hug and what doesn't. He wants to follow a good leader and please you. You'll be astounded at how well your dog can behave when taught well. Dogs are never out to get you or purposefully do something wrong; that is not how dogs' minds work. They always choose to please a calm, clear, confident leader, and choose the right behavior if they've been clearly taught it and had their needs met.

If you practice every day, use a lot of consistency and repetition, have very clear expectations, and proofed your work through distractions when you advance, success will come sooner. If you practice only at home without distractions, your dog won't learn how to behave in the real world. (You'll learn more about proofing and distractions in the next chapter.) If you practice only occasionally and briefly, your dog will progress slowly. If you are inconsistent, your dog will sometimes listen and sometimes not.

> Dog behavior that you do not like is usually a problem coming from you. If you are anxious, fearful, and unsure, you'll have an anxious, fearful, and unsure dog.

Believe me, this training can be a lot of fun and very rewarding. You'll be astonished how good it feels to watch your dog improve, and you'll love showing off your dog's skills and talents. Best of all, you *and* your dog will be happier!

5

STEP THREE—ADVANCING YOUR TRAINING

*If you're walking down the right path and you're willing
to keep walking, eventually you'll make progress.*
~Barack Obama~

Stages of Training

I have divided dog obedience-training into five stages so that you can see how to properly advance, slowly and one stage at a time. Make sure you fully complete each stage before moving on to the next.

If you have problems with any of the advancement techniques, see "Having Trouble?" (page 132).

Stage 1

1. No distractions, on-leash practice at home.
2. Your dog can demonstrate sit, down, and come.
3. Your dog can stay for 1 minute. You are immediately next to him, kneeling.
4. Beginning let's go no-pull walk, early stages.
5. Refining techniques as a handler and learning to read your dog's body language.

Stage 2

1. Once your dog understand the commands, add small distractions while he is on-leash.
2. Your dog can demonstrate the following commands on-leash, gradually increasing the intensity of distractions: sit, down, and come.
3. Your dog can stay for 2 minutes with small distractions, gradually increasing in intensity.
4. You stay close to your dog for sit, down, and stay, but you can now stand and command him. Increase distractions for the let's go no-pull walk and then move on to introducing a more formal heel.

Stage 3

1. You begin to move away from your dog, still using the leash. Maximize distractions.
2. Your dog can demonstrate the following commands on-leash with all distractions: sit, down, and come.
3. Your dog can maintain the stay while you move away. He can maintain a 5-minute stay while you are at the end of the 6-foot leash, with distractions nearby.
4. Your dog can perform the heel in position well, with distractions. He moves at your pace and turns with you.

Stage 4

1. Work with a 25-feet line (training lead), with heaviest distraction. Start this stage only after you've been completely successful with stage 3, using the 6-foot leash. If your dog is still being inconsistent with commands, do not move on to the long training lead yet. Similarly, if you thought your dog was ready but when you used the long line he started being inconsistent, go back to the 6-foot leash for a while.
2. Your dog can demonstrate all commands while you are 25 feet away, using training lead.
3. Perfect the heel.

Stage 5

You have off-leash control of your dog with distractions nearby. Your dog demonstrates all obedience commands while off-leash.

You and your dog should be very proud of yourselves.

When to Advance

It's not the load that breaks you down,
it's the way you carry it.
~Lena Horne~

Knowing when your dog is ready to move up in each level is tricky.

- Every dog is different.
- The amount of time each person puts into a dog is different.
- Every handler's skills are different.

You have been paying attention to your dog and learning to read his body language. That's the best clue for knowing when to advance. If your dog is following commands well, then you are ready to advance. Advancement can mean

- practicing near more intense distractions
- getting closer to distractions
- adding distance between you and your dog during obedience

If your dog is too unfocused, reduce the level of distraction. If being 5 feet from the squirrel is not enough, move 100 feet away from it.

Reducing a Distraction

As you begin adding distractions to your obedience routine, there are sure to be times that your dog starts to lose focus and you can no longer practice the obedience successfully.

To reduce the intensity of the distraction, move farther away from it and gradually build up your dog's ability to get closer.

This illustration may give you an imaginary reference point. The middle of the circle is the epicenter, or your dog's highest form of distraction at level 10. This is where your dog "loses it." As you know, your dog cannot learn in level 10, so you need to lower the level to regain focus. Say your dog is in a relaxed state, 500 feet away from the center of the distraction. The outer part of the circle is labeled 1, to represent the distance necessary for a relaxed dog. As you walk closer toward the center of the circle, your dog's distraction level increases.

Each step you take toward the middle, or the epicenter, raises your dog's level. If you start walking and your dog is still fine and under control at level 4, for example, you can keep trying to get closer to level-10 distractions. But if your dog loses control at level 6, go back to level 4 and regain control by putting more distance between you and the distraction. Then slowly move a little beyond level 5 and practice obedience just before you reach level 6, since that is where you know you lost control. You may have to stay at level 5 for weeks, depending on how much you practice.

When you sense your dog is doing well, start approaching level 6 again—there's a good chance your dog can handle it now. If you do lose your dog's focus, go back to level 5.5 and practice more obedience. Each time you practice obedience in the area just *before* your dog loses control, you teach him to take it to the higher level next time. You're slowly building your dog's ability to maintain control. If you do this consistently over time, one day you'll notice you can now go to level 8 whereas before you may have had to start at level 3! Maintaining control means you can walk your dog without pulling and he is still looking around and back at you. Losing control means he stops checking in with you and may be pulling or showing other signs of out-of-control behavior like yelping, whining, or barking.

Know your dog's levels of distraction and work up to them. Don't expect to be able to train him right next to barking dogs on the first day. Challenge both yourself and your dog, but do not do it too soon. Feel comfortable with each command and action before adding distractions.

Moving Up the Stages

When you have gotten to the point where your dog understands commands in the house and the training is going well, it is time to start advancing. This involves adding distractions and "proofing" your work. This kind of practice helps your dog listen to you even during times of heightened distraction.

Do not add distractions until you know your dog understands the commands. When you are home and you tell your dog to sit, he sits. When you tell him "Down," he goes down. When you tell him to come, he comes. You should also have been working on stay, so your dog is able to stay for a couple of minutes with you next to him. Remember, you are not holding him in the stay, but the leash and collar are relaxed and you are just near him in preparation to catch a break in the stay.

Distractions

Distractions are things your dog will look at or be focused on instead of listening to your command as he did when the distraction was not there. When your dog is relaxed, notice his body language. Observe how relaxed his tail, face, and ears are. His mouth may be slightly open. But when something gets your dog's attention, notice that his mouth generally closes, his ears go forward to listen to the distraction, and his body looks tenser.

If your dog displays this attention but relaxes again, then he is not too distracted. But if his tension builds and he doesn't take his eyes off the distraction, this is where you step in and change his focus.

Distractions to a dog can be any number of things:

- Other dogs
- Cats
- Squirrels
- Kids
- Birds
- Balls
- Smells
- Water spraying from a hose
- Things with wheels—cars, trucks, bikes, skateboards
- Sounds

Just leaving the house is a distraction because there is a lot of stuff going on in the world! Every dog tolerates each distraction in a different way. By now you probably know your dog's distractions and to what level they may affect him.

Purposefully using distractions in dog training slowly builds up your dog's tolerance and ability to behave well in all situations. He will be more prepared when he comes across all the distractions of the real world.

Let's say that Max goes crazy when he sees cats. If you do not practice this situation to help him learn control around cats, then every time Max sees a cat he will go into that crazy level-10 energy and you will not have control. So what do you do? Practice your obedience near cats, gradually decreasing your distance from them.

A level-10 distraction might be a cat right next to Max. You can reduce the level of distraction by moving away from the cat.

For example, start at 200 feet from the cat with Max's back to the cat. Once you've mastered that, have Max turn around and face the cat and do more obedience practice.

Your next step is to move a little closer to the cat. Don't expect to get next to the cat right away. This process might take days, weeks, or even months. It is important to move up your steps only when you and Max are both under control. If you get too close to the cat and Max cannot be brought back into control, it is better to move away from the cat and gain control again.

You should be in the mood to do this kind of distraction work. If you are tired or frustrated, do it at another time. Each time you do practice this, your dog improves, so that one day you will find you can just pass by the cat without incident. That is how it works. Practice and prepare your dog for the human world and he will move about happily in it!

Initially offer small distractions, like having a friend walk by your dog or throw a ball past him or make noises—just enough to gain some of your dog's focus so that you can practice getting it back. You don't want your friend to call your dog, as that can be confusing. Often just going out to your driveway is enough of a distraction in the early stages.

Over time, you'll notice that you can get closer and closer to the object of distraction while still maintaining control of your dog. This happens for two reasons: (1) your dog has begun to learn control around that object of distraction, and (2) you have built up more confidence in your skills and also a higher expectation of your dog.

If a dog has never practiced near a particular distraction, he probably won't be prepared for it. Plus, dogs can learn to be very obedient on certain streets because you've practiced on the same street a hundred times, but when you bring them to a new area they act like they don't know their obedience anymore. Practice in many different areas, so your dog is exposed to new smells, sights, and experiences.

Here are great areas to practice on-leash training when you are advancing your dog's skills:

- Near the entrance of grocery stores
- Inside pet stores that allow dogs
- Outside the fence near a dog park
- Near a field of children playing soccer
- On a new street, with new dogs in the area
- At a new park, near a busy playground full of children
- At a friend's house with her dog or cat nearby
- Near a favorite tree to mark

Some of you may be wondering when you will have the time to do all this work. You'd be surprised how much obedience you can get done when you make it a part of your daily routine during your walks. If you add a few 5- to 10-minute sessions every day, imagine how much time that is per week. Then, on your days off when you have more time, you try a half-hour session at the park or just before you go to the dog park. You *can* work it in and you'll be saving time and stress in the process. Imagine having a well-behaved dog!

As with all commands, advance slowly using increasing levels of distraction and practice a lot of repetitions in a lot of different areas and scenarios.

Advancing the Recall (Come Command)

When your dog always comes when you call him without distractions in your home, you can begin to advance the come by adding distractions. Get in the habit of doing it on your exercise walks too. Say you have released your dog to go pee on a tree. When you are ready to start walking again, take this opportunity to practice the come command to get him back to you. Practice it every time you want him to get to you, several times a day. Your dog will have fun getting to you for all that praise or treats.

Teaching a good recall requires a lot of practice in a lot of different circumstances and distractions. Your dog will be only as good as the amount of time you practice with him. Plan on practicing daily and taking your dog to new places as often as possible. Two of the most helpful areas to practice are in front of your door and around other dogs.

- If your dog ever accidentally runs out the front door, there is a better chance you can call him back if you have previously practiced there. Think about situations where you would like to be able to call your dog to you. Then practice in those situations so that you can have good recall in those spots.
- There are times when you will need to call your dog to you—if you notice another dog displaying unfriendly behavior, for example. You want to call your dog away to prevent an incident. Practice recall when your dog is on-leash around other dogs so that if ever you need to get him to you in the future, you can.

Plan on working several months on this command before you even think about beginning your journey to the off-leash command. Believe me, your diligence will be well worth it. Be sure to save the come command for on-leash right now, or you will ruin the word for your dog. If you are telling him to come to you off-leash and he gets away with not coming, you'll delay your success.

> The keys to obtaining really successful off-leash recalls are practice and dedication and not trying to jump up the stages too soon. Practice and patience will lead you to success.

You can advance to the next level, when your dog is coming to you *every time* you say come. Then you can begin adding more and more distractions for proofing and advancing your training. Once your dog is coming to you at all times within your 6-foot leash range and with distractions, you can use your long line of 20–30 feet and practice with him farther from you. Remember, do not do the off-leash until you have succeeded with the long line.

If your dog is off-leash and not coming to you, do *not* go get him. A chase game only reinforces that it is more fun to have you chase him than to come to you. Instead, walk away after the first call and entice your dog with silly sounds. If your dog is properly bonded to you, he will want to come to you. When he gets to you, praise and/or treat. Do not get angry with him for not coming the first time, because he will interpret this as you being angry at him for coming to you *this* time. If your dog has disobeyed the command, he is not yet ready for the off-leash level.

Always make it an extremely positive experience to come to you in all ways. Teach your dog that when you say "Come," not coming to you is not an option. When he gets to you, he receives a lot of praise and a happy leader!

Advancing the Let's Go No-Pull Walk

To advance the let's go walk, begin by passing by distractions. As you approach the distraction, make sure your dog's focus is on you and not the distraction. To accomplish this, it is a great idea to begin obedience right in your driveway or on the sidewalk. Practice sits, downs, stays, and comes with your dog before you begin your walk. Then make sure your dog is walking next to you and not pulling or walking too far ahead of you. If you start the walk with your dog focused on the distraction, you will have a harder time redirecting his focus, so it makes sense to start the walk with the focus on you.

Get as close as you can to the distraction without losing control of your dog. Move farther away to regain it. When you are out on a walk, challenge yourself and your dog by gradually increasing distractions. If your dog always has a problem in a certain area, work on it and practice it until it gets better. Next time he will remember that he learned control in that area and will be able to do it again and even better.

It is fascinating that when a dog walks through a neighborhood and is out of control, all the other dogs there begin to bark and carry on. If that same dog walked through the same neighborhood but under control and not in an anxious state, all of the other dogs would be calmer and most would not even bark. It is true! They communicate with signals. You may find that when your dog is better trained, your neighborhood walks will be quieter.

Advancing the Sit, Down, and Stay

Sit

You are ready to advance your sit command by adding distractions only if your dog *always* sits upon command without distractions. Here is an example of a sit with distractions:

1. Say your dog's name and then say: "sit." If your dog's ears and eyes are pointing toward something that is distracting him, try enticing him with a treat to perform the sit. If that fails, increase the distance from the distraction and repeat until you succeed.
2. Build up to the big distractions over time. Work on the smaller distractions, then add more and more as you both feel ready.
3. Praise for that act of sitting. Make your dog feel good about pleasing you. Practice patience and calm, clear, consistent leadership and you should do well.

Down

Begin advancing your down command by adding distractions when your dog performs a down *every time* without distractions. Example of a down with distractions:

1. Say "Spot, down" with your hand gesture, as learned (page 108).
2. If your dog does not respond and is distracted, entice by showing a treat. If that fails, reduce distraction and build up to it with practice.
3. Repeat the steps until you are successful.

Stay

Down-Stay

After you have mastered a down-stay while squatting next to your dog and he can maintain that stay for a couple of minutes, it is time to gradually increase distractions. Stay close to your dog when adding these distractions. You can go out on a walk in your neighborhood and ask your dog to stay on the sidewalk with a distraction in the distance. Practice this daily for a couple of weeks.

Remember that you are the one who releases your dog from the stay. Don't let your dog decide when to release.

After your dog really understands the stay command and does not try break the stay by getting up, you can begin to stand up while still next to your dog. Repeat the stay to your dog before you stand up or move away from him, or he may take it as a signal to stand up with you. You should still be standing right next to your dog for stays when doing this level of training. Practice standing next to your dog near distractions over a period of days or weeks until your dog is always successful with distractions before you step away.

When your dog does quite well with you standing next to him without breaking the stay, it can be time to take a step or two away.

1. When you take the step away, repeat "Spot, stay" or he will think he should go with you.
2. Make sure the leash is loose while you are walking away; you don't want to tug him accidentally.
3. After just a few seconds, repeat the stay command, then return to your dog with lots of praise.
4. Repeat.

Gradually increase the time you are staying at a distance from your dog while he maintains the stay. Every time your dog looks at you to check in, make sure you praise for that. It will confirm to your dog he is doing the right thing and you are happy with the stay.

If your dog breaks the stay often, stand next to him again to have better timing. When he understands well over time, you can move away again.

TO TEACH A RELIABLE STAY:
1. Slowly add more and more distractions.
2. Watch your dog very carefully for signs he may break the stay, and catch him before he stands up with a quick "No, stay" and put him back into the stay.
3. Praise your dog for checking in with you, especially if he looks at you.
4. Slowly work up to 10 minutes or more of a stay, starting with 1 minute at a time over a period of weeks to months with daily practice.

When your dog is in a down or down-stay, expect him to lie there without rolling over or reaching to sniff something or eating grass. If you allow him to do one of those things, he will likely forget the assignment. Keep the sessions serious.

If at any time your dog is breaking the stay and getting up, go back to the beginning and move closer to your dog. It is most important to have good timing for this to be successful.

Sit-Stay

The sit-stay advancement is the same as the down-stay except your dog is in a sit position. Remember, your dog is not comfortable sitting for long periods of time, so keep this stay under 5 minutes or so.

If you are having problems with any of the advancement techniques, see the section "Having Trouble?" (page 132).

Heel

In a heel position, your dog is next to you on your left side. Your dog's right ear is parallel to your left leg just next to you. He can be standing or sitting (see photo on next page).

You define where you want the position and teach your dog that position. If he is too far ahead of you, he will not see your movements, so the best position is his head directly next to your leg.

After you have practiced the let's go no-pull walk daily over several weeks or so, your dog should be improving and understanding where you want him on a walk. When your dog understands where he is supposed to be and you are having success with distractions, begin increasing expectations and call this formal position: "Heel."

A good heel means your dog watches you closely and follows your every move at your side. If you turn, he turns; if you speed up, he speeds up; if you stop, he stops. It is like a dance.

Surprise your dog with your actions. If he pulls ahead of you, quickly turn in the opposite direction and give praise when he reaches the desired position. Change your pace often, praise when he is doing well.

As with all advanced dog training, you add distractions to proof training while your dog is on-leash. You do not ask for this heel off-leash until you have mastered the on-leash.

Having Trouble?

Life's problems wouldn't be called "hurdles"
if there wasn't a way to get over them.
~Anonymous~

Are you having trouble with something during training? See if you can find the cause so you can resolve the issue and move on.

Take a break, step back, and look at the situation logically. Take a deep breath if you are feeling frustrated. Break it down.

- Are you meeting your dog's physical needs? If he has pent-up, unreleased energy, you will have trouble training him.
- Are you meeting your dog's emotional needs? Do you spend enough time together just hanging out or playing? Your dog needs to be bonded to you.
- How is the timing and sincerity of your praise? Maybe your praise or corrections are a little too soon or too late. Has your dog been feeling rewarded for good behavior?
- Have you practiced this particular situation enough? New environments with new distractions take time to get used to. Perhaps the distraction level is too high for your dog at this point and you should build up to it.
- Are you moving ahead too quickly? Many people who have problems getting their dog to obey commands find they need to slow down. Perhaps you didn't make things clear enough for your dog before you moved on to higher distractions. Practice patience and repetition.
- Are you practicing regularly and being a calm, clear, consistent leader? If not, your dog will not be consistent either. Take a few steps back and begin again.
- Are you experiencing extra stress in your life that your dog can sense and is affected by? Practice the destressing techniques I described in chapter 3.
- Are you having one of those crazy days when you are agitated about a lot of different things? Take a break and come back to it when you feel better.

Evaluate Your Timing and Technique

The timing of your praise and your corrections has to be instantaneous. If your timing is even slightly off, this can affect your dog's progress. If your dog is breaking the stay, for example, go back to the beginning and work on the stay closer to your dog. Then gradually introduce distractions. If your dog is popping all the way up before you stop him from breaking the stay, be faster with your timing to stop him. Before your dog stands all the way up, stop him with a quick "No, stay" and put him back in the stay.

If your dog jumps up on the counter for food and actually gets the food before you stop him, then your timing is off. He got the reward and so is likely to do it again. Stop him the instant his paws hit the counter, before he even tastes the food. How can you be so quick? Or what can you do if it happens while you are in another room? Set up the situation as practice. Put some tempting food on the table and get your dog on-leash and stand next to the temptation on the counter. Don't encourage him to jump, of course, just stand next to it and pretend you are busy with something. You can even walk him past it a few times. If he leaves it alone when you pass, praise him. If he starts to go for it, instantly say "Leave it." If he actually jumps up to get it, say "No, leave it!"

If you are having a really hard time stopping your dog from getting food off the counter, try using a loud sound to make it uncomfortable for him to do it again. The second he goes for the food, toot a kid's bicycle horn or something. The sound should be perfectly timed. The second his nose goes for the food, you create the loud sound. The sound should startle him enough that he does not want to do it again.

Setups like this give you the opportunity to plan for your dog to make a mistake and have great timing when he does because you are prepared. In the case of the food on the counter, he probably won't make that mistake again because your timing was so good. Use setups for getting into the garbage can or anything else he is not supposed to do.

Are You Practicing Enough?

Have you called your dog to come to you and he didn't come? Practice on-leash in the area where he didn't come. Go back to the beginning by practicing with your 6-foot leash and build up to the 25-foot distance using your long line, gradually adding distractions as your dog progresses.

Don't avoid situations—use them to learn! Say your dog always goes a little crazy when the mailman comes. Next time, be prepared and use that as an opportunity to advance your dog. If you just avoid it every time, he won't learn. While you are on your next walk, think about all the opportunities you have to expand your dog's abilities. Use those opportunities to train your dog well.

Evaluate Your Leadership

Is your dog generally not listening to you? Go back and think about what kind of a leader you are being for your dog. Are you calm, clear, and consistent? Does your dog clearly understand your rules? Are you being fair with your expectations of your dog? Are you showing frustration with your dog?

Evaluate Your Dog's Needs

Are you fulfilling your dog's needs? Is he getting walked enough and tired out at least twice a day to the point he lies down to rest? Are you spending enough time with your dog? Is your dog having playtime with other dogs? Is your dog healthy and having regular checkups with your veterinarian?

Follow Your Intuition

Pay attention to what your gut is telling you. Slow down and really listen and trust your instincts. The solution is often already within you.

> *Follow your instincts. That's where true wisdom manifests itself.*
> *~Oprah Winfrey~*

If you are sure that you have been doing everything right and your dog is still not behaving in the way you want him to, you have two options. You can contact me through my Web site and we can discuss your concerns directly. Or you can contact a local in-home trainer to help you.

Stay motivated, you can do this! I know you can.

Off-Leash

Do not attempt to do off-leash training until your dog is responding to *all* commands under *all* kinds of distractions on-leash. You may start advancing to creating off-leash control only after you've mastered on-leash. When your dog is on-leash, you have the proper timing and technique to teach him well and for him to completely understand. If you try to do off-leash training before he is ready, it will not be reliable.

Prior to using a long line for the stay command, you first need to succeed by being at the end of your 6-foot leash (see photo on next page).

After your dog has been doing very well with you immediately next to him during distractions, you can begin stepping away to the end of your 6-foot leash. Work on this training until your dog is doing well before advancing to the longer line.

Down-Stay

1. Ask your dog to go into a down.
2. While standing next to your dog, say his name and the command: "Spot, stay." Walk to the end of your 6-foot leash and repeat "Stay."
3. Watch carefully.
4. Praise your dog when he looks at you or toward you.
5. Repeat stay command occasionally.
6. When you approach your dog again, repeat "Stay," then approach.
7. Release and praise.

Repeat by adding distractions and requiring your dog to maintain stay for longer periods of time. Remember, your tone for commands should be firm and low, and your tone for praise should be softer and higher pitched.

The Long Line

Now that you are at the end of the leash about 6 feet away from your dog and are having success with your dog's response, it is time to use your long training lead.

The long training lead is just an extra-long leash. I suggest you use a 20- to 30-foot training lead (see photo on next page). It allows you to move far away from your dog to practice commands such as the recall and stay, and even to start teaching off-leash trail walks. With the extra-long leash you can teach these commands at a distance and perfect them so that you can move on to off-leash.

The long line should not be the retractable kind. You do not want your dog to feel you reeling him in, either. He should do the job because this prepares him for the feeling of being off-leash. You do not want your dog to feel tension on his neck during practice with the long line. It is used to test if your dog is ready for off-leash.

A long training lead is made from a cloth material. Tie a few knots in it about every 5 feet or so. This will give you leverage for holding on to it, and if the lead is dragging on the ground you can put your foot on it and the knot will catch on your foot rather than slip under (if you are trying to stop your dog, for example). At this point, you should be using this training lead only when you are feeling fairly certain your dog will listen.

It is a good idea to keep your regular leash with you initially when you begin to work with the longer line. If your dog is failing a lot, you can revert to the 6-foot leash for more practice.

Try the long line in all kinds of situations where it is possible for you to be up to 20 feet or so away from your dog. Continue to add distractions and practice your commands like the come and stay when you are at the far end of the long line. Tell your dog to stay and walk to the end of the lead. Now your training is similar to what you've been doing at the end of your 6-foot leash, but you have added distance. If your dog is breaking the stay or not coming when called, go back to the short leash to practice more.

Off-leash Trail Walks

Walking your dog on a trail that allows off-leash dogs can be a wonderful experience for both of you. If you have progressed well in training and your dog is under control around other dogs, people, and even other animals, you can begin to imagine life with an off-leash dog.

My dog Fax's favorite thing is off-leash hiking. He loves that sense of freedom while we explore nature together. But I did a lot of recall work to get to that point with him. With dedication and some practice, you can have that too.

While using the long line, initially teach your dog what sort of distance away he is allowed in preparation for when he is off-leash. This can vary, but I don't recommend a distance longer than about 15 feet or so in the beginning. Imagine how close you want him and teach him that. When your dog goes farther away, use a command like "Keep close." Praise when he is in the area you want him to be and call him back to you if he gets farther than you allow. Your dog will learn the accepted distance fairly quickly if you are consistent on the first few walks and you praise him when he looks at you to check in.

Your dog can be wherever you allow him on these types of walks. If he goes off the trail and that is not okay with you, call him back and show him where he is supposed to walk. Just be very clear and even give it a name, like "this way," or you can point out the direction with your hand. Make sure you are praising your dog when he is back on track and when he checks in with you on his own. If your dog has traveled ahead of you and looks back at you, give him praise for checking in.

Your dog should not be pulling on the long line. It should be loose so he does not feel tension; otherwise he will not be prepared when you take it off for off-leash walking.

If your dog has not checked in with you for a while or appears very focused on something, this is a great time to do recall work. Say "Spot, come." Praise when he reaches you, not before. Make that praise a very exciting big reward. Ideally, you'd like to see your dog's tail wagging and some eye contact. If your dog gets to you but doesn't really pay attention to you, that isn't the ideal recall. You want him to focus on you.

Continue to add distractions to proof your recalls on the walks. Be sure your dog has had experience calmly passing by other dogs and hikers, and that you can call him to you whenever needed.

Removing the Long Line

Before you remove the long line, let it drag to the ground without you holding it for a period of time. This is your final phase before removing it. Do not remove the long line until you have successfully mastered all commands in all kinds of distractions. Remove the long line only when you are completely confident in your dog's commands. This is how you will have very successful off-leash control.

If you've trained your dog well up to this point, he is responding to your commands quickly and *every* time. The line at this point is there in case he doesn't listen. It is a test. If he listens to your commands every time with the long line dragging, then it is time to remove it and officially have an off-leash-trained dog.

Congratulations! Off-leash control is a fantastic tool to enjoy your life with your dog even more. An off-leash-trained dog can enjoy many benefits and you should feel really proud of yourself when you reach this stage.

6

BEHAVIOR MODIFICATION

Behavior modification is a specialized area where you are trying to change a behavior that is unwanted rather than just teach a new behavior as in obedience. You may also find it helpful to work with me through my Web site if you are struggling with a behavior problem you need resolved.

Feeling Frustrated with Your Dog

> *When you come to the end of your rope,*
> *tie a knot and hang on.*
> *~Franklin D. Roosevelt~*

Frustration is a continuing sense of dissatisfaction arising from unresolved problems or unfulfilled needs. It is human nature to get frustrated with your dog from time to time. It can come from disappointment that you didn't get what you wanted, or from an obstruction in your path toward your goals.

Frustration can get in the way of seeing everything quite as it really is. It can be like trying to see through a heavy fog, hampering your ability to continue on your path to reach your goals.

Here are ways to help lighten your frustration.

Write It Down

What exactly is frustrating you? Try to be very clear about the main source. Are you feeling frustrated every day about this issue, or are you having a particularly bad day because you are tired, overstressed, or something totally unrelated to your dog is bothering you? Be very specific about your source of frustration. Some examples: Did you come home to find that your dog destroyed something? Has your dog seemed to forget commands? Has that been happening every day, or were things going well for a while? Evaluate what has been happening lately that could cause the change. Have you been practicing obedience as a calm, clear, consistent leader every day? Has your routine or environment changed? Did you walk your dog today? Is your dog picking up on extra stress you are having? Sometimes when you break down the situation it can be clearer how to resolve it.

Reread and Possibly Redefine Your Goals

A goal without a plan is just a wish.
~Antoine de Saint-Exupéry~

Go back to your goals (page 76) and try to determine where you started, where you are, and where you want to be. What can you do now to get you back on track toward your goals? Is there something you can do differently this time that may make you more successful? Are you meeting your dog's needs? If not, then chances are you won't reach your goals. Think about ways you can work his needs into your schedule. If you haven't been walking him every day, ask yourself why. Are you too busy? Then work out a schedule that makes it happen and make it a priority. It will be good for both of you. Are you physically not able to walk him enough? Hire a dog walker or a teen in your neighborhood, or ask a friend for help if you need it. Remember, you are working on reducing your frustration, so asking for help may be a good solution.

Keep Track of the Goals You Have Reached

Even though in this moment you may be feeling like everything is failing, it isn't. We all go through good times and bad, and so do dogs. One day your dog may seem to understand something and then the next day he doesn't. This could be due to many different factors. Write down where you started and what you *have* accomplished so far. It can help to see what goals you have reached or what areas have improved so you can feel good about going forward. It can also help to figure out what areas you need to improve. Say, for example, your dog is really good at sit but is not consistent with coming when called. Have you practiced come as much as sit? When you are frustrated, it can be a little gift to make you aware of what to spend more time working on.

Visualize What You Want

Be clear and positive. Positive thinkers often reach their goals more easily and more successfully. If you are a procrastinator, work on ways to get going. Perhaps making a list of what you want to accomplish each day and a box to check them off can help. I am a big list maker. Once it is written down and posted, I feel I have to do it. It feels really good to check off the boxes too!

Create Balance in Your Life

Make a list of all your responsibilities for the day, the week, or even the month, and create balance by prioritizing them. What works best for me is the opposite of procrastination and—I am very driven to action. This can be a drawback if sometimes you can't stop yourself until a task is completed and the rest of your life gets out of balance. Lists help keep me centered and balanced so I work everything into my life that is needed.

Take a Walk

Exercise releases hormones in your body that make you feel good and is one of the most natural and effective cures for stress, anxiety, and depression. It is good for both you and your dog.

Relax

Go back and reread "Feeling Stressed or Overwhelmed?" (page 63). Often feeling stressed with your dog is more about feeling overwhelmed by life in general. Take a break. Do not train your dog when you are stressed out. Find your balanced center and work through all the steps before you begin again.

Remember that your dog isn't purposely frustrating you. He just isn't always sure what he should and shouldn't do.

Excessive Barking

Dogs usually bark out of boredom, habit, or both. The first step is to prevent it. Determine if there is a cause and if you can prevent the barking knowing that cause. For example, if your dog barks at the same thing at the same time every day, can you distract him then or avoid the particular situation? Also, make sure your dog has been well exercised every day so that his physical needs are met. Excessive barkers may need to be walked at least three times a day. Your dog likes to leave the house and do things so he doesn't get bored. After you are sure your dog's physical and mental needs are met, try the following to stop the barking.

1. Stand in front of your barking dog with a treat in your hand. Ignore your dog until he has stopped barking, even for a split second, probably to smell the treat. The second your dog isn't barking, say "Quiet" and give the treat.
2. Repeat.
3. The idea is that your dog starts to understand that the second he is quiet he gets a treat. Never give the treat while he is barking.
4. Again standing in front of him with a treat, this time say "Quiet" while he is barking. Treat the second he is quiet.
5. Be calm and patient and do not yell or get angry—or your dog will think you are joining in on the barking!
6. Continue this for several sessions over a few days.
7. When your dog is automatically being quiet when you give the command, slowly start to increase the time you expect your dog to stay quiet from, say, 2

seconds to 4, then to 6, and so on before giving the treat. Say "Quiet," then delay giving the treat for a couple of seconds.

8. This method may take time, but it is one way for you to work on the barking problem right away. It also establishes the meaning of the command to your dog so that after a while you can just say "Quiet" and he will stop.

9. Take your dog for a walk a couple of times a day or more, so that his energy is drained and he feels content at home.

If you have trouble getting your dog to stop barking in order to give the command, you can fill an empty can with a few pebbles, marbles, or dried beans and tape it shut. Shake it to make a loud noise. This is often enough to startle your dog to stop barking for that second to start your process of teaching the quiet command.

One of the many positive things about dogs is that their past behavior doesn't prevent them from changing. In fact, if you decide that from now on your dog is not going to be an excessive barker, you can make that happen. Don't think about his past, focus on the now.

Barking for Food

If your dog barks when you are about to feed him and then you set his food bowl down, you have just reinforced the barking.

Being calm and quiet is the proper way for your dog to wait for his food. From today on, things can change. Put a leash and collar on your dog and ask him to sit-stay while you prepare his food. Practice this daily, and if your dog isn't very good at it, practice it in a quiet environment and work up to doing it during the food preparation (which is more dif-

ficult for him) when he fully understands the command. This is another example of how obedience training is very important.

Your dog should sit and stay while you are preparing the food (see first photo on opposite page). Hold the food bowl in front of him and wait until he is quiet before putting it down. If he jumps on you, turn around and ignore him. The second he stops barking, put the food down. Now he is rewarded with food for being

quiet. If your dog is doing well, go a bit farther in your training and ask him to sit-stay while you put the food bowl down and expect him to wait a few seconds until you release him (see photo above, right). This is an excellent way to work on the stay! If he goes for the food before you release him, pick up the food and start again. Be sure to praise your dog while he is staying well and being patient, so he knows he is doing a good job.

You must be *very* consistent for this to work. If one day you put the food down when he is barking, you've destroyed all the other days you worked hard at waiting until he was quiet. Dogs are very smart. If you are sure of what you want from your dog, and you practice it every day and you are very consistent with it, you will have success. If you give in one day because you are tired, you will not be successful in the future. It takes time and energy initially, but when done well it becomes easier and easier, until one day you forgot it was even a problem!

WAYS TO TEACH THE QUIET COMMAND
- Startle your dog quiet with a loud noise, like shaking beans in a can.
- Turn your back on your dog to ignore him.
- Leave the room so you are not offering the attention he is seeking.

Try different things and see what works. In my experience, improving behavior and having a well-behaved dog can be easy if you meet your dog's needs, practice daily obedience, and are calm, clear, and consistent.

Extreme barkers must be kept busy, active, and regularly practicing obedience. When they are not being trained, manage the environment to help avoid their specific triggers. If your dog barks outside, he should not be left in the backyard and instead kept indoors, unless you are there to correct the barking. If he always barks at the UPS guy, for example, then when UPS comes, he should have his attention refocused either doing obedience or brought to another part of the house. The idea is that you begin to consistently stop the barking and your expectations of your dog are very clear.

Working with your dog with obedience is a great way to make your word mean something to him. If you have been doing obedience with your dog and he sees you as the leader and trusts you, then you can just tell your dog to stop barking and that works. Many things can be improved when you

- meet your dog's physical and mental needs.
- do obedience training daily.
- are consistent with distracting your dog to stop the barking, praise when not barking.

Barking in the Car

Sometimes the easiest solution is prevention. Many people find that putting their dog in a crate covered by a sheet in the car prevents barking because he cannot see all the things that normally make him bark. Over time you can try to remove the sheet. Praise and treat for quiet. Replace the sheet when he barks. He should get the idea that he is rewarded for being quiet. Eventually, you won't need the crate either and he'll just enjoy the ride without the barking. (Exercising him *before* the car ride helps too.)

Barking Through the Fence

If your dog barks through a fence

- don't leave your dog alone in the yard without your supervision to stop the behavior.
- create a fenced-in area that he can't see through.

Behavioral problems cannot be fixed if your dog is not being exercised properly to drain his energy 2 or 3 times a day at least. So that is always step one of every solution.

★ Barking Q & A ★

Q *Jack is an 8-month-old Weimaraner and we are having some problems with him barking—for attention (?). We take him out LOTS, so he is exercised, but often he just barks and wants us to give him attention (spoiled?). If we ignore him, he keeps barking. I'd like to ostracize him, but to where? He is good in his crate so I don't want to send him there. If I give him attention, then he continues to expect it. He gets plenty of attention from us a lot of the time and he has all kinds of toys and chews. We can't constantly entertain him if he is bored?! He also barks for food. Please help.*

A Barking for attention is a common problem. Dogs learn really fast, and the one time they barked and got rewarded with food or attention they learned that was how to get what they want. Stopping this behavior takes patience, but with dedication and consistency you'll be able to do it. As long as your dog has been properly exercised and worn out, you can resolve this problem.

First, take a big portion of the day and work on this consistently. Say, for example, you are sitting on the couch and Jack barks. Here are the steps to follow:

1. Get up and leave the room, close the door behind you. Don't say anything and don't let him follow you. This tells him that he loses your attention when he barks.

2. After his barking has stopped, enter the room and sit back down on the couch.

3. After you sit down and notice Jack is not barking, make sure to give him attention and even treats.

4. If he barks again, repeat the process by leaving the room again as in step 1.

This method is very effective but it may take you leaving the room 10 times! If you do it consistently, it will work. If you give in even *one time* with his barking, you undo all your previous work. If you are very consistent with this for the first week, he'll get it and your problem will be resolved.

The same thing goes for barking and eating. If Jack barks before eating and then you give in and feed him, he has just been rewarded for barking and will bark more next time. It is very important that barking is not rewarded and instead results in losing you and your attention. He should be waiting quietly before you set down the food bowl.

For this process to work you have to do it every time. Just keep in mind what your long-term goals are. Walk away with no attention and no words and no eye contact. He doesn't want to lose you so it will be his motivation to stop.

It is great that you keep him exercised. He is reaching his "teen" years and will need all the exercise he can get. If he is the high-energy type, which it sounds like he is, completely tire him out several times a day, the kind of tired where he is panting heavily and flops down to rest when he gets home. If he is still following you around and up and about when you get back from the exercise, you know it wasn't enough for him. Weimaraners love to swim—they have webbed feet!—and fetch, so these are other great ways to tire him out.

★ Excitable Barking Q & A ★

Q *I have an 8-year-old red heeler–beagle mix who is an excitable barker. I love to take Molly to the local dog beach, but she just runs around and barks at all the other dogs, especially when they are playing ball with their owners. She is fine when I put her on the lead, but that kind of defeats the purpose of being able to run around at the beach. She is also fine when there are no other dogs at the beach. I would love to stop this problem so we and all the others who love the beach can have a peaceful time there.*

A Lucky dogs who go to the beach. How fun! Molly is so excited at the beach that she doesn't know how to control herself. That's why she goes into the barking frenzy. I suggest that you practice obedience before you even let her off the leash. With obedience you'll be teaching her how to have that control. This can give her a chance to calm herself before she goes into her frenzy.

Do positive obedience a distance away from other dogs and slowly build up her control by moving closer. Practice as far away as you need to be to get her focus on you and then over time work closer and closer. Molly must have her attention on you during the obedience; if it isn't, move farther away until you have her attention. When you do decide to let her off-leash again, practice recalls and obedience intermittently to get her attention. Watch her closely, and if she goes into that excited state again, get her back on-leash, move a distance away, and do the obedience. If you are getting her attention often, you'll help to prevent that frenzied state.

Over time, she'll learn that she can control herself, please you, and have a good time all at once. It can take time to work on this, and you won't solve it in one trip to the beach, but with practice and patience you can teach her to enjoy herself, and you will feel a lot happier too.

Jumping

One of the most common problems people have with their dogs is jumping all over guests. You want your dog to be friendly and happy to see people, but you don't want him knocking over your elderly father in his enthusiasm.

The key to fixing this problem is to teach your dog to associate greeting a person with a calm, sit position. It takes patient practice, but this can be done and the results are wonderful. The basic idea is that you set up situations for your dog to practice over and over until he is ready for a "real" greeting. Follow the steps below.

1. **Teach a good sit on command.** Stand near your front door. Hold a treat in your hand and ask your dog to sit: "Spot, sit." Give the treat as soon as his rear end hits the floor. When your dog is consistently sitting for you, wait a second, then 2, then 3, etc., before giving the treat. Over time he will learn to sit a little longer before receiving the treat.
2. **Have your dog sit on a mat near the front door.** Get a mat for your dog and place it near the front door in the spot you would like him to sit during greetings. Keep treats near the door and practice showing your dog to the mat, have him sit, and then offer the treat. Give it a name, like "Go to your mat." Repeat until your dog consistently sits calmly on the mat.

3. **Practice the entry.** Bring treats with you, leave the house, and reenter. Ask your dog to sit on the mat when you enter and treat him when he sits. Be calm and consistent. When your dog is doing well, you can add the knock on the door or ringing the doorbell before entering.

4. **Invite a friend.** Now that your dog is consistently sitting on his mat and patiently waiting for his treat, invite a friend over to help you further practice your dog's ability to do a proper greeting.

As you can see, you intentionally set up circumstances for your dog to learn and to be successful. He will soon understand that a calm greeting offers a delicious treat! Eventually, when your dog is doing really well, you can begin to offer the treat only every other time, ultimately replacing it with sincere physical praise. So sometimes he performs the greeting and receives a treat, and sometimes enthusiastic petting.

Instruct visitors not to pet your dog during a greeting unless your dog is calm and not jumping. If your dog jumps on guests, ask them to turn their back and ignore him. If your dog sometimes receives attention when he jumps, you will not get him to stop. But if you never allow jumping, he'll learn this quickly.

When your dog is not jumping, it is very important that you reward him for it every time, either with a treat or with genuine physical praise. As with all training, it is important to make sure your dog is receiving enough exercise. At least twice a day, take your dog out for exercise to the point he is tired out when he gets home. A dog with too much pent-up energy will not be able to learn a proper, calm greeting.

Fence Jumping

If your dog spends a lot of unsupervised time outside, you'll need a fence. Your dog's breed, size, athletic abilities, and motivation to explore the world determine how high the fence should be. A good rule of thumb: higher than you think.

There are exciting things outside the fence—sights, sounds, smells, noises, people, other dogs, cats, squirrels . . . All this is much more interesting than being alone behind the fence, and your dog may try to jump over. It is not enough just to have a fence he can't jump over. You don't want your dog jumping for hours and being frustrated. He may also be barking all day, and you need to prevent that (see "Excessive Barking," page 143). There are ways to deal with this.

Is your dog getting enough exercise, 2 walks a day for at least 30 minutes each, lying down to rest when you return? Is he getting out to explore the world enough? Dogs who do not get enough exercise often jump the fence because they are bored and want to get out and explore. For a short-term solution, your dog can be indoors with you or supervised while he is outside until you have time to establish clear rules.

Dogs who are left outside alone a lot, without sufficient exercise can often find almost any way of getting out, or causing destruction if he can't get out. Even if the fence is too high for jumping over, if you do not meet your dog's physical energy needs, you may not solve your problem.

Additionally, if you have not spayed or neutered your dog, do so now. An in-heat female or intact male will do almost anything to get out to breed.

If your dog does jump the fence, do not punish him when he returns. He doesn't know that jumping the fence is a bad thing, and in his mind you'll be punishing him for *returning*.

You can train your dog not to jump. Positive obedience training is the key to getting your dog to understand what is acceptable and what isn't. Your obedience training should be consistent and effective so your dog trusts you and believes you know what you are doing, so he tends to listen and follow the behavior you prefer.

Here are guidelines:

- Exercise your dog daily. A tired dog is a good dog.
- Spend quality time with your dog. Do not leave him alone outside. Supervise while he is outside.
- Neuter or spay your dog to prevent him or her from wanting to escape to breed.
- If you are gone for long periods of time, consider a doggy day care or a dog walker.
- Obedience-train your dog through a positive program so you can more effectively teach him your rules.

Destructive Chewing

In the world of dog behavior, destructive chewing of your furniture, shoes, and other belongings is a big no-no. Although the problem is equally troublesome whether your dog is young or old, the solution is a bit different for puppies than for adult dogs.

Puppies

Chewing is a normal part of growing up, because all dogs explore their environments with their noses and mouths, and because puppies are teething. Just like human babies, puppies have to gnaw and chew on objects to help cut the new teeth through the gums. Until your puppy has learned what he may and may not chew, keep things away from him that you don't want him to have, and don't allow him into areas of the home that are not puppy-proofed unless you're there to supervise. It is important that you offer your puppy appropriate chew toys to help him through this phase and that you train him to use them. Keep a suitable chew toy near you at all times so that when you catch your puppy mouthing something he shouldn't have, you can quickly redirect his chewing to the more appropriate item.

You must actually catch your puppy in the act to train him successfully. When you see him chewing on something he is not supposed to have, use a command such as "No chew," take the item away, and replace it immediately with the toy. Offer lots of praise when your puppy takes the toy.

Never yell at, hit, or spank your puppy for chewing or for any other reason. He will lose trust in you and is likely to develop more serious behavioral problems.

Prevention, correct timing, redirection, and genuine praise are the keys to successfully preventing destructive chewing in your puppy.

Adult Dogs

In adult dogs, destructive chewing is usually the result of boredom, loneliness, separation anxiety, and/or lack of sufficient exercise. Dogs require plenty of time with their humans, including lots of physical exercise and mental stimulation. Before you leave for work, make sure you've exercised your dog well and do so again after you get home.

Most dogs do not like being alone all day. They prefer an active, busy life. If you cannot give your dog the time he needs, try doggie day care or hire a dog walker to come by a couple of times each day.

How do you know how much exercise is enough? Your dog should lie down to rest after a walk because you have worn him out. Practicing obedience training daily is a great way to mentally stimulate your dog.

Do fun activities together, such as hiking, biking, pet therapy work, search and rescue, agility, flyball, herding, etc. Find out about your specific breed's natural interests and try something new.

As with puppies, punishing your adult dog for destructive chewing only adds to your problems. If you catch your dog chewing something inappropriate, simply redirect his behavior to something he is allowed to chew. Have appropriate chew bones and toys available at all times and praise your dog when he uses them.

MORE POINTERS

- To give your dog something good to chew on while you are away from home, there are specially made chew toys that can be stuffed with kibble.
- Never punish your dog after the fact. If you come home and find something destroyed, there is no effective correction. Yelling at or spanking your dog will only confuse him and damage your relationship.
- Your dog isn't destroying things to "get back at you" or because he is angry. This isn't how a dog's mind works. Dogs want to please you. If you meet your dog's physical and mental needs and show consistency through appropriate leadership, you can successfully eliminate destructive chewing.
- Whatever his age, spend a lot of time with your dog and provide lots of love and guidance. This is how dogs learn right from wrong.

- There are many options to improve your dog's life, and the effort will be well worth the reward of having a happy, healthy dog who isn't destructive.

★ Destructive Dog Q & A ★

Q *I have a 3-year-old rat terrier I adopted from the humane society 2 years ago. Stimpy has eaten 5 sofas and 20+ bed pillows since I got him! We crate when we're not home, but he will rip up the furniture even in front of us. Often, there is a deer or a person in the yard and he gets excited and grabs and shakes whatever is nearby. My veterinarian recommends medicating him, which I don't want to do. We love him so much and want him to stop. I don't know if he was abused in his prior home, but if we raise our voice to him, he just collapses on the floor and covers his face with his paws. So scolding him isn't an option. Please help Stimpy! I know he wants to be a good boy.*

A If Stimpy rips up things when he sees a deer or another person, those things must set him off. I would say that he is experiencing some sort of anxiety when he sees those things, as if the sight of them excites and overstimulates him, and his way of handling it is to rip things up. Panic and discomfort can be at the root of the destruction. Dogs have different ways of relieving pent-up feelings; some bark, jump, or dig, and others rip up furniture. Knowing why Stimpy feels this way isn't necessary to resolve the problem. And the things in his past can be left behind when new, positive experiences replace them. There are several things I suggest to correct it.

Most important, Stimpy needs to get really tired out at least twice a day, every day, through a lot of exercise—to the point that he lies down afterward. This is the first step in correcting the problem. If he hasn't drained his pent-up energy through daily exercise, he won't be calm enough to learn. If Stimpy spends too much time in his crate without enough exercise, the chewing will be harder to correct.

He should leave the house and view different scenery and people and animals every day to build up his tolerance to various stimuli. Take him to a different park or down different streets on your walk. Dogs who go outside and experience different smells and sights do better overall because this "opens their minds" so they aren't as panicked or excited by stimuli they see from home.

I recommend having Stimpy on-leash, attached to you while at home for a couple of weeks to improve the timing of stopping the behavior and to give him something to do (he will have to pay attention to whoever has his leash and follow wherever he or she goes). Just attach the leash to your belt, and Stimpy has to go where you go. When Stimpy begins to show signs of ripping something, you can immediately stop the behavior and replace it with another behavior. Timing is most important here; if you wait even a few seconds to stop the behavior, that is too long to correct it. When he is on-leash with you, you'll be able to stop the behavior immediately.

There are two good ways to replace the behavior:

1. Distract Stimpy with something else, either a toy he is allowed to have or a bone to chew on (here you are showing him what is allowed in his mouth).

2. Second, practice obedience, like sits and downs, when he is experiencing anxiety. This will build his tolerance to the circumstance as well as his confidence. Use treat training, not physical punishment training. When you use good obedience during a stressful time for a dog, it can change the way he sees that stressor. Instead of it being a stressful event for him, you will have retaught him that he *can* handle it, and it will make him happier *and* save your furniture.

Separation Anxiety

Separation anxiety begins *before* you leave your house. Your dog wakes up with energy that needs a release. If you leave the house without giving him some way to release that energy, he may have separation anxiety issues. You have to really tire him out, so he is in a quiet state when you leave. For medium to large breeds, add a dog backpack. If you cannot do a walk in the morning, put him on a treadmill while you get ready, or hire a dog walker (see "Exercise!" page 80, for more info). Then, after he's had some good exercise and a bit of rest, feed him, which will make it a lot easier being quiet the rest of the day.

Be calm when leaving and returning. If you have a big good-bye or an overly excited return, it may increase separation anxiety. Help your dog be calm by remaining calm when you leave or enter. Your dog senses your anxiety. If you have exercised your dog well and plan to again when you return, you don't need to feel guilty, so don't let your dog sense

your own anxiety about leaving him. If needed, you can practice obedience with him to get him in a calmer state. Then, when you are ready to leave, don't talk to your dog, don't pet him, and don't look at him while you are leaving. If you've exercised your dog and fed him prior to leaving, he will naturally be quieter and ready for a long nap.

Go out and come back into the house many times before you really go out for a length of time. Pretend you are just going out to get your mail or something like that so you don't project an anxious feeling. Plus, if you have gone in and out without your dog many times, he will not know if you are going to the garage and back or if you are leaving for the day. Also, dogs pick up on your habits. The noise of your keys as you head out the door can be a signal to him you are leaving. Try to do all your practice exits the same way.

When you return home, don't offer a lot of attention to your dog in the first few minutes. Walk in quietly and act as though you had been gone briefly. Then, after a few minutes of being home, take your dog out for a walk and afterward give him lots of attention when he is in a relaxed state. The idea is that your dog should not know if you are going to the car to get something or if you will be gone all day. You should leave and enter with very little notice of him.

Follow this process:

1. Start by leaving the house for 2 minutes, 5 minutes, then 20 minutes, 40 minutes . . . over a period of several days to weeks.
2. Make sure your dog is well exercised before leaving so that he is in a natural state of rest.

3. Don't make a big deal out of leaving. Don't be emotional in saying good-bye or hello. Just walk out and walk in, without any attention on him.
4. After you've been back for a few minutes, then you can give your dog quiet attention. The point is, you don't want your exit or return to cause any kind of anxiety. It is just relaxed and calm.

If your dog follows you around everywhere, give him some practice being away from you. You should be able to close the door and be on the other side of it. This gives your dog a chance to learn how to be alone.

Provide stimulating things for your dog to do while you are away. You can hide his food all over in different areas so he has to "hunt" for each kibble. You can stuff a KONG with peanut butter (you can even freeze the peanut butter in the KONG overnight to make it harder or stuff kibble within the peanut butter). There are similar products that you can fill with food so your dog has to work to get it, which keeps him busy and stimulated.

Submissive Urination

To understand why your dog is doing this it helps to understand dominance and submissiveness in the dog world. In situations where an overly sensitive dog feels intimidated and excited, the response is to urinate to show that he recognizes the other person or dog's dominance. It is common for this to happen during greetings. It is *very* important to understand that punishment makes the situation worse and he is not doing it on purpose or out of spite. In the dog world, this is proper behavior. But because he is living in the human world, you understandably want to change the behavior.

First, make sure that your veterinarian rules out any physical problems. After that, move on to controlling the behavior. For submissive dogs, positive reinforcement for good behavior is very important to build their confidence. I suggest an obedience plan that uses treats, favorite toys, and other positive motivators.

Greetings are usually the main culprit. Upon arrival, both you and guests should ignore your dog for the first few minutes to minimize the excitement that leads to the urination. This is hard when your cute dog is excited to see you, but it will be better in the end for both of you if he doesn't pee on the floor. You can resolve this problem if you handle it carefully initially. Just walk in calmly, with no eye contact and no petting.

If your dog has not been out to eliminate for a while because you have been away, head straight outside to allow your dog to urinate to decrease the chance he will do it indoors. Just walk past your dog and act as though he is not even there, open the door, go outside, and your dog will probably follow you. If you are expecting guests, make sure your dog has eliminated outside before they arrive.

After the excitement of the arrival has ended, acknowledge your dog in a calm way. When you do pet him, do not stand over him, as this is a sign of dominance. Sit calmly and let him come next to you. Ask all guests to do the same.

Over time, your dog won't get so overwhelmed with the greetings and his behavior should be controlled. Make sure you are exercising your dog regularly and having him relieve himself often and especially before you are expecting guests.

Positive obedience programs build confidence in your dog as well, which may also reduce the submissive urination. Keep practicing your daily obedience.

Greeting Other Dogs

It's good for dogs to spend time with other dogs. In the dog world, dogs learn to meet and greet and play together appropriately. But dogs who live with humans often need to be taught.

★ Teaching Your Dog to Greet Other Dogs Q & A ★

Q *My dog Coal is a Lab/pointer/pit mix. He is extremely intelligent, very well behaved, and good with other dogs. But when the leash is on, he has a bad habit of pulling, barking, and whining when he sees another dog in the distance. I want to be able to pass by other dogs on our walks without him "losing it."*

A It sounds like you are describing what I call "leash frustration." Dogs with this problem are fine when they meet dogs while not being restrained by a leash, but as soon as the restraint is there, the problem arises. Your dog may be lunging at the end of a tight collar and leash wanting to get to something. This kind of frustration can lead to aggression. Some trainers who do protection training actually want to create aggression and they do so by using a tight collar and leash. Knowing this, it is *extremely* important that when dogs greet one another they do so with a loose collar and leash.

I also highly recommend using a head collar to walk Coal so that there is no tension on his neck and you have more control on the walk.

Teach Coal to calm down in stressful situations. If you are out on a walk and he is approaching other dogs that will trigger the barking and whining, teach him to follow you and turn away from the other dogs. Have a treat ready and put it near your dog's nose, and when he begins to follow the treat, make a turn away from the other dogs in the distance. Use your let's go command at the same time. Give Coal the treat lure after he has completed the turn.

Your aim is to avoid the frenzy of the sight of the other dogs, by having Coal follow you and turn himself in the opposite direction. Then you can continue walking in the opposite direction or put him in a down-stay with the other dogs behind him so he is not focused on them. Continue this for several minutes until Coal's body begins to relax. This also teaches him that he can learn control in stressful situations. Over time, he can learn how to be calm near other dogs and you can work up to being able to walk past them calmly.

Additionally, you can teach a where is it? command as well, where essentially you are training Coal to look away from the object that may lead to the frustration (in this case, another dog). Drop a treat on the ground and ask "Where is it?" in an excited tone. After he eats the treat and comes back over to you, give another treat. The goal is to have your dog looking down for the treat and then focusing on you so that he is not paying attention to the distraction you are trying to avoid. Do this several times until Coal is very focused on you. Keep this up until he is consistently focused on the treat or you and then walking with you on-leash. It is very important that Coal does not feel tightness on the collar, so keep the leash loose.

The aim of these exercises is to teach Coal to turn his attention off of oncoming dogs.

You, as the leader, should feel relaxed and calm when Coal is passing another dog, and his leash should be loose so he does not feel pressure on his neck.

Leash frustration can be neutralized with these techniques, good obedience, and a dog learning his proper role in the family.

Mouthing Behavior in Adult Dogs

Mouthing is normal with puppies, and it can take time to train them to stop. Adult dogs that mouth do so because they have not been trained otherwise. It is very important to train all dogs that their teeth do not belong on your skin.

★ Mouthing Behavior Q & A ★

Q *Three weeks ago I rescued a 2-year-old female Pyrenees mix. Her former life was basically on a chain. My problem is that Zoe weighs 60 pounds and is very mouthy, like a puppy. When she gets excited, she tries to grab us. She also has an issue of jumping up. She does not jump on us; she just leaps up off the ground with all four legs (like a spring!). She seems very eager to learn and to please. She is housebroken. I keep her in a crate when we are not home. She has plenty of chew toys, and we are quick to reprimand her when she steals anything that isn't hers. I heel her when we walk (still learning, but doing well). I just don't know how to stop the mouthing! I have 3 other dogs and they all get along well. She seems to follow their lead and is learning quickly. I think she acts more like a 6-month-old than a 2-year-old!*

A Thank you for adopting a rescued adult dog! It sounds as though Zoe has a lot of pent-up energy. Here are steps to follow that can help you with her mouthy behavior.

Step 1

First and foremost, make sure she is exercised really well at least twice a day, every day. Exercise is the key to fixing most problems because even if you have a perfectly trained dog but do not drain her energy, you'll begin to have problems you can't fix.

Step 2

Begin a regular positive obedience program with Zoe so that she learns how to control her behavior and also that you are the leader, which will make her listen to you better. Obedience is a great tool when she is in the overly excited state too. For example, when you sense she is becoming too excited, stand up, put her leash on, and begin obedience practice. That changes the mood to a working mode and she'll learn how to focus her energy. When you do the positive obedience, Zoe will receive the attention she seeks through rewards like praise and treats. In this sense you both win: She gets the attention she wants from you, and you get a better-trained dog.

Step 3

If you are in a moment when you cannot get a handle on Zoe's mouthing behavior, there are a couple things to try:

1. When her mouth goes on you, stop all play and quickly say "Ouch, no biting" and give her a chew toy to occupy her mouth instead. When she takes the chew toy in her mouth, praise her and give her attention. If she again goes for your skin, repeat the process.

2. If offering her a chew toy as an alternative doesn't work, then the best idea is to remove yourself instantly and go in another room without her. She then loses you as her playmate. After a minute or so, reenter the room and try again.

3. Repeat the process until she is no longer displaying the bad behavior. It is important to reenter and give her another chance. To stop the training on a good note, keep leaving and reentering as many times as it takes her to get it. If you practice this a lot right away and you are really consistent with it, Zoe will learn quickly.

If you are not consistent and allow the mouthing behavior occasionally, she will never learn to stop. But if you decide from this moment on that she is not allowed to do it and you follow my steps, you should be successful very quickly.

Ball Obsession

Most dogs have a favorite toy, and often it is a ball. Balls are fun to chew, push around with paws or nose, chase, and catch. But when a favorite toy becomes an obsession, it is time for human intervention.

★ Ball Obsession Q & A ★

Q *I have a 3-year-old Pom/Yorkie/Maltese mix. He is obsessed with balls. He would play fetch 24 hours a day if only he had someone whose arm wouldn't give out. The problem is that when my son tries to play with any type of ball (football, baseball, soccer, etc.), Wicket goes nuts. Even if my son is outside playing, Wicket barks his head off and jumps on the door trying to get out. I usually end up shutting the inside door and closing the blinds so he can't see out. What can I do to get him to know the difference between his fetch time and my son's playtime?*

A I feel for you because my own dog Fax had a stick and water obsession when we first adopted him. When anyone had a stick or was running the water with a hose, he too "went nuts." He would fixate on it and have to have it. There is a solution, although it takes practice and patience on your part.

Most dogs who are trained well through obedience behave and do pretty much whatever you want them to do because they have learned to "trust and respect" your commands. Obedience is a form of communication between you and your dog. It gives you the tools to teach your dog what you expect from him in a way that he understands. When done well, obedience is a lot of fun for your dog and it is very rewarding. Your dog will benefit from learning the obedience command leave it. This command teaches your dog to leave alone whatever you asked him to.

The next step is to make sure Wicket understands which balls are his and which ones are not. This is done through practice. For example, Fax has toys that he knows are his, and he knows that the children's toys are not his. How does he know the difference? He was told "leave it" whenever he went toward the toys that are not his. When he did leave the toy, I'd quickly offer him physical praise or a treat and give him a toy he was allowed. Your timing of the command and your timing of rewarding for leaving it are very important for Wicket to learn it well.

Work with the leave it command during intentional setups while he is on-leash with just a few balls at a time. You must be *extremely* consistent for this to work. If he is allowed to have a certain ball one day and not the next, it will just confuse him. But if every time he understands which balls are his and which ones he is not allowed to touch, he'll learn quickly.

One of the most important steps to resolve your problem when your son is playing outside is refocusing Wicket's attention on something else, through obedience, to stop the obsession before it starts. When your son is going to play with a ball, be ready and work with obedience like a down-stay *before* he starts. When you notice Wicket begin to lose concentration, start to ask him for more commands, like sit, down, come, etc. In that intense moment you are asking him to pay attention to you through different commands and not focus on the balls. This is a way to make him calmer so he doesn't reach that have-to-have-it stage. These are precious seconds just before your dog reaches the crazy stage, so intervene and change his focus by giving him something else to do.

If you wait too long and Wicket reaches that wild stage, it is very hard to refocus him. Watch his body language and learn how to catch him before that moment begins. The idea with refocusing is that it teaches your dog a way of being calmer, to take his eyes off the balls, and relax. Teaching a long down-stay is very valuable here. If you release Wicket from the obedience and he starts to get too worked up over the balls again, go back to the obedience. If your timing is good and you are very consistent, over time your dog will be more relaxed and calmer around your son playing with balls nearby, and you'll be very proud of yourself too.

Apprehensive Dogs

Worry never robs tomorrow of its sorrow,
it only saps today of its joy.
~Leo Buscaglia~

This quote is more for you than your dog. It is natural to worry about your apprehensive dog, but doing so won't resolve things; it will only be harder on you. Instead of worrying, try to respond and act on what needs doing. Remove your worry and you will be able to see more clearly and your dog will trust you sooner. Remember, you are the calm, clear, confident leader, not the worrier.

Fearful dogs can be scared or nervous about all sorts of things: loud noises, other dogs, strangers, trucks, children, etc. Some fearful dogs simply run and hide, while others express themselves through aggression. Dogs who have behavioral problems caused by fear can often be reconditioned or desensitized and improve. It can be a long process that requires patience and consistency and a lot of hard work on your part. If your dog has already bitten, I suggest you work with a trainer in person who has experience with this type of fear-based behavior problem. Make sure you ask for references and hire someone who has specific experience with aggression.

If your dog is fearful of something, try to associate that object of fear with something he likes. This can be done using rewards.

FIRST THINGS FIRST

1. Drain your dog's energy daily. Fearful dogs benefit from good old-fashioned exercise! Wear out your dog every day and every time before you begin practice.
2. Think about what your dog fears and write it down. Keep a journal for a week or so and note very specifically what you notice he fears. Be very clear: Is he scared of all loud sounds, or just the vacuum or thunderstorms? Does he fear all unknown humans, or just children or men in hats?
3. Once you have a good idea of what your dog is scared of, you can start working on improving it through a process of desensitization, either with distance or reduced sound so that you decrease the intensity of the situation to a point he can handle. The goal is to change your dog's association with that fear to something he now remembers he gets rewarded for. So instead of fearing the object or sound, he associates that object or sound with a reward.

Desensitizing Your Dog

Step 1

Let's say your dog is scared of the vacuum cleaner. Arrange for your dog to notice the vacuum but is not scared yet. For example, take your dog outside, where he can see the vacuum through a window but he is safe. Have someone turn on the vacuum inside. The second the vacuum goes on, treat your dog.

Treat him only if he is calm, not if he is bolting away, barking, or showing other behavior that is out of control. You want to take your dog to a point where he notices the vacuum but is not scared—that is when you treat. If your dog is still afraid, move farther away from the window and give the treats while he is noticing the vacuum but not reacting.

Here's another example. If your dog is scared of bicycles, set up a situation where someone has a bicycle far in the distance. Find the point where your dog notices the bike but is not scared. Treat at that moment.

Keep practicing the scenario over and over for days or even months. Do not go closer to the object or increase the intensity of the sound yet. Your dog needs a chance to change the way he perceives the object—as something he feels good about because of the treat.

When your dog's response to the object or sound is excitement for the reward, it can be time to move on to step 2. First, make certain your dog is responding with excitement in all situations you can think of. Practice with a different bicycle on a different street but the same distance. When you feel certain your dog no longer views that object with fear on any street, you can move on.

Step 2

Gradually move closer to the object or increase the sound. For example, have someone turn on the vacuum when your dog is in a different room, or open the window to the outside and then turn it on. Practice the same way with treats. When you are successful, gradually move closer to the vacuum until, hopefully, your dog can be in the same room with it. This takes time.

For the bike, gradually move closer. Over time, your dog should be able to be near the bicycle without fear. The vacuum and bicycle are examples; just about anything your dog fears can be approached in a similar way. By doing things gradually and changing your dog's association with the fear to a positive (the reward), you'll be increasing your dog's ability to handle the situation.

This step may take weeks or months to accomplish. Just take a few minutes every day or even every week to practice. If you avoid scary things, your dog will not get better. A few months of work now will result in years of a happier dog and a happier guardian. I've noticed in training that sometimes when you work on one thing you actually improve several other things without even realizing it.

SUMMARY
- Exercise your dog daily.
- Learn your dog's specific fears.

- Desensitize with a reward at a distance until he is comfortable and not showing fear.
- Practice, reward, practice, reward, practice, reward!
- Gradually increase intensity.
- Don't treat if your dog shows fear.
- Be patient.
- Reward yourself for the little things.

If you are the guardian of a dog who was abused in the past and is showing signs of extreme apprehension, a positive obedience program is an excellent way to help him. Apprehension often comes from confusion and lack of confidence from past abuse. Positive obedience with calm, clear, consistent communication will help your dog to learn what is expected of him. Rewards for good behavior will build his self-confidence. It takes time and patience on your part, but I've seen excellent results.

> In time of difficulties, we must not lose sight of our achievements.
> ~Mao Tse-tung~

For extreme situations, you may want to contact an in-person trainer who is knowledgeable about abuse, or you can contact me through my Web site for more assistance.

Apprehensive Dog Barking and Housetraining Q & A

Q *I'm fostering Tootsie, a schnauzer who was rescued from a puppy mill. She's 5 years old and starting to come to me to sniff my hand. She gets along famously with my other 2 small dogs. But I have two issues: (1) Tootsie barks at any noise, and then the others start. How can I calm her down when she is still apprehensive of me? (2) How can I help her with housetraining when I can't physically put her outside if I catch her in the middle of doing it, as she runs away from me?*

A Luckily the things in a dog's past can often be left behind when new, positive experiences replace them. There are several things I suggest to correct it.

Barking is often an indication of isolation, fear, frustration, or boredom. Dogs—even nonbarkers—do not do well left alone for long periods of time. Your dog must be exercised a lot, at least twice a day every day. A tired dog is a good dog and will most likely spend a lot of time sleeping if her needs have been met. Apprehensive dogs especially benefit from being gradually exposed to more stimuli and require exploring new sights and smells.

Make sure you praise Tootsie and give attention when she is not barking. If you mistakenly give her attention when she barks, it will reward the behavior, and if you forget to give her attention when she is quiet, you are missing out on an opportunity to train her not to bark. I highly suggest you begin an obedience-training program using positive methods to build up her confidence as well.

Because Tootsie is apprehensive of you, I recommend having her on-leash, attached to you, while she is in the home for a couple of weeks or so, so that you can perfect the timing of stopping her barking and so you're giving her something to do (she will have to pay attention to whoever has her leash and follow wherever you go). Praise or treat her often to encourage and reward good behavior and to build her confidence even more.

When she barks, teach the quiet command. Hold a treat, say "Quiet," and give the treat when she is quiet. This rewards her for not barking.

Regarding the housetraining accidents in the house, most of fixing this issue is about education and prevention. Dogs who eliminate in the house may be doing it out of habit or they may simply need more training. Rule out physical causes with your veterinarian.

1. Clean all areas she may have messed in and remove the odor with an odor neutralizer you can find at the pet store.
2. Observe input and output when she is outside peeing or pooping.
3. Get to know her body language right before she needs to eliminate—circling, sniffing, etc.—so that you can bring her out *before* she has the accident.
4. If there is an accident, secretly make a sound to startle her to stop and then bring her immediately outside to pee, and praise outside while she is peeing.

Be vigilant about observing and preventing. The effort you put in now will pay off. Tootsie should not have free access to the house until the accidents have stopped completely. Then, allow access only to the room you are in and observe closely. If there are no more accidents inside, you can slowly offer more of the house. At this point it is a lot about prevention on *your* part to fix the problem.

When Tootsie has had no pee accidents in the house for several weeks, you should be able to practice having her off-leash again but supervised closely initially. If there is an accident, go back to the beginning and have her with you at all times.

★ Fear of Thunderstorms Q & A ★

Q *Maggie, our sheltie, is 5 years old. Her owners (second set) said she barked at thunder and ran along their fence. Well, that was an understatement! She charges toward the sound, barking and trying to "attack" the noise. She seems to be totally focused on going after it. She has been on several antianxiety medications without success. When we see a storm coming or hear thunder, we quickly crate her with the radio on and a chew bone to distract her. This is pretty successful, but I worry about times we aren't home. We live in a rural area, and she is outside unfenced. It never is a problem until thunder comes. She is not aggressive to people or other animals.*

Maggie's other issue is unexplained nervous behavior. For no reason (or a reason known only to dogs) she will run toward a plant and jump to tear pieces off it. She also twirls, paces, and appears agitated. This isn't constant and you never know when it'll happen. She has been on medication for almost a month now and I do see an improvement, but I hate to think she'll need medication all her life to be seminormal. It does nothing for the thunder.

Do you have any suggestions on how we can help her? We are used to her routine and so are our neighbors. I just feel sorry for Maggie.

A It sounds like you have done a lot to help Maggie already. It's great that you have found that crating her with the radio on and a chew bone is something that helps. Since the crate has been successful for you, is it an option to crate her with the radio and chew bone when you are away from home and expect a storm? Or perhaps leave her in a room with no windows and the radio on? I highly suggest you don't leave her outside during the storm if she is so fearful of it.

Your attitude can influence the severity of Maggie's fear of the storm. If you are nervous during storms, your dog senses that. Or if you comfort Maggie by petting or saying it's okay in a soft voice, she interprets that as being correct for having a fear of the storm and it reinforces the negative behavior. Plus, it is natural as a human to feel sorry for her, but try not to display that to her. She interprets that as you thinking something is wrong with her, which only makes her feel worse. Do *not* punish her; this may increase her anxiety.

STEPS TO REDUCE FEAR

1. Exercise Maggie daily and even more on the days that a storm is likely. The exercise will help tire her out and is even thought to increase serotonin levels, which can have a calming affect on your dog.

2. Do not comfort or punish your dog during storms.

3. Provide a safe place. Some dogs prefer an enclosed space like a bathroom, bathtub, closet, or a crate. If Maggie feels comfortable in a crate, you can cover the crate with a blanket.

4. Try to block the noise of the storm by running a fan, TV, or radio. Sometimes putting the dog in a room without windows helps.

5. Maintain your strong, calm leadership attitude and try not to feel scared or nervous yourself. Use a happy voice; it would be great if you could get Maggie to play during a storm!

6. Try behavior modification techniques to help change Maggie's response to the storm. You can provide her favorite treat, toy, or game just prior to a storm, and that is the only time she gets it.

7. Practice obedience training and reward Maggie when she does something well. Do not reward when she is anxious or scared.

8. Try desensitizing the noise of the storm by using a CD of storm sounds. Play the sound at a lower level at first and gradually increase the sound until your dog gets used to it. If Maggie starts to get scared, decrease the volume. Try it in different rooms too, and if successful play it sometimes when you are not in the room with Maggie. When she is successful and not showing signs of fear, you can repeat once a week or so. Then, when there is a real storm, do the same thing with the same obedience or tricks and rewards that you did for the CD noise. It is usually a good idea to practice the desensitizing when there isn't a real storm, so try to do it before storm season so you have a chance to practice before the live event.

9. Talk with your veterinarian about medications if needed.

Regarding the nervous behavior and attacking the plants, is Maggie getting exercised enough? Often dogs who display this sort of behavior feel better when they are *really* tired out more than once a day. Exercise to the point that she has to lie down to rest. This helps to drain stored-up energy, release her body's hormone serotonin, help her relax, and generally offer her mind and body what she may need.

Additionally, try to divert Maggie's nervous behavior with positive obedience. When you notice signs of nervousness, work on positive obedience so she can refocus onto something constructive.

★ Desensitizing a Fearful Dog Q & A ★

Q *I recently rescued Attley from continuing her job as a puppy mill mom for the past 4 years. She is a gorgeous golden retriever who is leery of everything and everyone other than my boyfriend and me. I understand this resulted from the breaking of her spirit at the mill and I understand that she doesn't know she is a dog! We have had to teach her to walk on a leash and eat out of a bowl and not be scared of the TV or the rain or other daily occurrences that you wouldn't think would be traumatizing. She is content to lie around all day rather than interact with us or her toys. We take her on about 7-10 walks a day, each averaging 20 minutes. We do not have a yard, so several of these double as potty breaks.*

Attley gets spooked very easily—leaves blowing down the street can send her running. As we were walking her this evening, we passed by a couple of kids and they said hello, and Attley began to pull. This happens all the time when she gets scared. However, this time all 74 pounds of her pulled me completely off my feet and she raced about 6 blocks heading for traffic. She ripped a nail out of her rear paw, and by the time my boyfriend caught her she was ready to stop and just get home. This is the second time bolting has happened in a week. What can I do to help her trust her surroundings on a walk and let her know that she is completely safe with us? I love Attley to death and want nothing more than to show her how much fun the world can be with her as a functioning dog. But I feel like I am failing her when the simplest thing can terrify her so badly that she will run into oncoming traffic.

A   You are *not* failing Attley! It sounds like you have already given her a great gift and have
    done a lot to help her. Take one day at a time and celebrate the small achievements.

It is important to let go of your feelings of guilt or worry or even feeling sorry for her. Dogs can be retaught and so it is important that you do not confuse her by feeling sorry for her. Take deep breaths before you go on walks and be as calm as you can be. She will sense when you are nervous and feel sorry for her, and that will make her feel like you are not in control; this, in turn will make her more nervous.

You can definitely begin a desensitizing routine with her as well as a positive-only training program. The training program can build her confidence and the desensitizing can help her adjust better. Desensitizing requires a lot of time and patience and is sometimes a very slow process, but it can be very successful.

STEPS FOR DESENSITIZING

1. Identify what triggers Attley's fear. Write down all the things that you can think of: loud noises, bicycles, kids, etc.

2. Begin to expose her at a very low level to whatever scares her. Some dogs are afraid of things with wheels, so if, for example, she is afraid of bicycles, then begin to introduce her to a bicycle with the bicycle very far away and still. If Attley is calm when she sees it, reward her with treats and praise.

3. Gradually move the bicycle closer to her, all the while praising and treating for calm behavior that does not show fear. If she begins to show fear, move the bicycle farther away and start again.

4. When she is comfortable with the bicycle, move it back far away and have someone ride it very slowly. If she remains calm, have the bicycle go faster and eventually closer.

> When your dog is showing signs of fear, *never* praise, pet, or treat in that moment or you are rewarding fearful behavior. It is human nature to coddle and hug when someone is scared, but if you do that to your dog you can actually make it worse for her by telling her that being scared is okay.

You are slowly increasing Attley's ability to handle the fearful object. This process may take days or even months, and should be done very gradually to be successful.

Practice obedience while Attley is being desensitized. If you are introducing her to the bicycle that is far away, have her practice a sit and reward for the sit. This obedience will get her to focus on something other than the fear and soon the reward of doing a good sit will replace the fear. She will begin to associate the sight of the bicycle with feeling good, proud, and happy because she got a treat and praise for performing a sit well.

Positive obedience with motivators like treats and praise does wonders for fearful dogs, increasing their confidence and lessening their fears. Don't use corrective obedience, which just makes them more fearful.

Dominant Dogs

If you want the most successful relationship with your dog and a dog who trusts you and is happy, do obedience training. In order for obedience training to work, you must be a well-established leader. A dog will listen well to you only when he trusts you and sees you as his leader. It is hard for some dogs to see you as leader. If you are having difficulty with your dog being dominant, is a good idea to add a few more tasks to your daily obedience routine.

Make the rule that from today on, nothing in life is free. This means that your dog should earn the one thing that is most important to him—food.

Prepare your dog's food and carry it with you for a bit until your dog is very hungry and following you around. Do not just put your dog's food bowl down. You want him hungry and following you for the food. Give only a few kibbles at a time when your dog has done something to please you. In this way, he will get his food over a period of time and be looking to you for the food. He will focus on you and see you as important to him. Go about your normal routine and stop occasionally to offer some of the food. Call your dog to you, give food, ask him to sit, give food.

If your dog barks at you or demands the food, immediately ignore him and definitely do not give it to him in that moment.

This accomplishes two things: (1) Your dog sees you as being very important, because you have the food and he is hungry; the leader provides food. (2) Your dog has to work for the food and earn it; this increases his respect for you.

Make sure you are also doing your daily obedience routines.

Aggressive Dogs

Most aggression should be handled by working with an in-person trainer who has experience with aggression. Ask to see references and make sure he or she has this type of specialized experience. Not all trainers do.

Dogs need a calm, clear, consistent leader in their life whom they trust and respect. A good leader has clear rules for the dog to follow in everyday life and doesn't allow aggression or any behavior leading to aggression.

There are usually stages that lead to aggressive behavior. If you can recognize these, you may be able to curb the process and stop aggression from happening.

STAGES LEADING TO AGGRESSION

1. Your dog focuses very intently on something, ears forward, body stiff, and he doesn't take his eyes off the object. You cannot easily get your dog's attention, and if you allow him to focus too long, he won't respond to you at all. Begin prevention here by practicing obedience with your dog to regain the focus on you.

2. Your dog begins to show anxiety by yawning, panting, and/or whining, and may become sensitive to touch. He may raise his hackles (the fur on top of the back). Try to remove your dog's focus from the object as quickly as possible in a calm and confident way. Do not show fear, frustration, or worry; your dog will pick up on that and the situation will get worse. It is a good idea to have your dog turn around so he cannot see the object and practice a down-stay. Maintain the down-stay for several minutes until your dog's body begins to relax.

3. Your dog looks at an object out of the corner of his eye (someone approaching his food bowl, or out on a walk when he is focused on another dog, etc). You can actually see the whites of his eyes, since he is generally not looking straight at you or the object but instead looking through the sides of his eyes.

4. Your dog may run away or attack.

Aggression During Greetings

In a *good* dog greeting, dogs approach each other from the side and smell each other's face and rear end, then continue on to something else or to play. The warning signs of a *bad* greeting are dogs stiffening and freezing, with their tail raised or their ears pinned back. If you notice these signs, call your dog back to you to interrupt what could turn into an aggressive display. You have to pay close attention and learn your dog's signals very well.

The stage just before aggression can sometimes be improved simply by practicing good obedience with your dog that establishes you as the leader and takes the leadership role away from him. But some forms of aggression are very serious and you will need a specialist to work with you. Seeking a trainer who specializes in aggression may be the best option in certain situations. You know your dog the best. If you fear your dog, it will be difficult to work with him properly and you may need to see an aggression specialist.

A dog who is properly socialized will learn not to act aggressively. Dogs tend to teach each other what is acceptable and what isn't. But sometimes this socialization period gets skipped as a puppy, so your dog doesn't get to learn. If you can find a dog that gets along well with other dogs and can teach your young dog what is acceptable and what isn't, that can help a lot.

Dogs have their own socialization experience, just as you do. Dogs know what way to approach each other that is acceptable and what way isn't. But if a young dog with the best of intentions goes zooming into another dog to greet him, he may be disciplined by that other dog because the greeting wasn't appropriate. This is what happens in the wild, and it can be a good thing—the dog learns that wasn't good behavior. However, this can be a bad thing if the dog doing the teaching is not good socially and has his own aggressive issues. It is a good idea to have your dog meet other dogs who you know are well socialized.

It is important to make this socialization period go well. You do not want your dog to feel frustrated when greeting other dogs with a tight leash. In addition, do not scream, yell, or be scared or angry at your dog, which can cause more problems. Study dog behavior and learn what is good and what isn't.

Causes of Leash Aggression

- You unknowingly reinforced the behavior when it first began by petting your dog when he growled or started showing preaggressive signs. You may think you are consoling him to make him better, but to a dog, you are signaling that his feelings of aggression are good.
- Your dog gets to greet other dogs only on-leash and pulls and barks to get to them. This is a completely unnatural way for dogs to greet each other and may

even signal to other dogs that your dog is aggressive (even if he isn't at that point), which makes the other dogs send threatening signals back. This can escalate into aggression.

- You show your own nervous anxiety or even fear through your breathing and by pulling back and tightening the leash, causing pressure in your dog's neck, which he interprets as a signal to get anxious and worried.

THE SOLUTION

1. Relax and stay calm when you are walking your dog.
2. Keep your dog's leash loose, and if he is a puller, use a head collar instead of a neck collar.
3. Do not pet your dog as a way of calming him. You should pet him only when he is already calm.
4. Change your dog's focus and don't let him pull you toward other dogs. If your dog is aggressive, he should not have contact with other dogs at this point.
5. Improve your leadership abilities through obedience training.

If you know your dog is not good with other dogs and has shown aggressive behavior, it is better not to greet other dogs and use prevention techniques instead. Unless you've worked with a specialist and he or she has taught you otherwise, teach your dog how to pass by other dogs, as I will teach you below.

Aggression is a dog's reaction to what he sees as a threat. Several things can cause aggression. The most common cause is fear. Another cause is frustration, when your dog is lunging at the end of a tight collar and leash and wanting to get to something. This kind of frustration can lead to aggression. Here it is better not to let your dog focus on the object he wants to get to and instead do obedience with his back to the object of frustration until you can gain control. Only after you have gained your dog's focus do you allow him to move toward the object and only if he is walking in a controlled, obedient manner.

It can be dangerous when your dog thinks he is leader. He can think he gets to make all the decisions, and if he sees you as in the way, it can lead to aggression. Our human world is not set up to have dogs as leaders. Being a leader is a very frustrating, scary, stressful, and difficult job for dogs in our world, and it almost always leads to behavioral problems. I cannot stress enough how important it is to be your dog's leader.

Another cause of aggression can be a dog feeling that he has to protect something, whether it is you or his territory or his stuff (toys, food, etc.). If you are leader and protect him, he no longer needs to be territorial. When you release him from this heavy responsibility, you reduce his stress and change the course that may have led to aggression.

Some dogs also respond aggressively when their natural prey drive kicks in from seeing something they consider "prey," such as squirrels, cats, cars, etc. When your dog's natural instinct to chase these things comes into play and he is allowed to focus too long on these objects, he may respond with aggression. It is important immediately to remove his focus from the prey and gain control over your dog with obedience practice. When you take the focus off the object, you stop the process that leads to aggression.

Aggression is a process, and if you can learn what triggers your dog, you can sometimes prevent it from reaching the full progression, by using obedience. In all these situations it is imperative that you be the leader in your dog's life. I have discussed how to be that leader throughout this book; now is the time to start to change your dog's life and your own for the better.

Encourage your dog to need you (see "Dominant Dogs," page 172). Make sure your household is very structured and that you are a clear leader. You can hand-feed your dog and make sure he knows you "own" everything, all toys and all food. Work with good obedience training daily so your dog learns very clearly to trust you and respect you. You can play hide-and-seek so your dog has to find you and is always aware of you.

Dogs communicate with each other in ways so subtle we often do not even detect them. Some dogs who were taken away from their mother too young or were not socialized properly at an early age haven't had the chance to recognize these important cues. This can cause other dogs to react negatively to your dog.

Dogs do not normally approach each other in a straight line, but when they are on-leash and pulling with chest out, you often force that straight line, which can actually cause other dogs to feel threatened. When a dog is feeling challenged, he can send signals that escalate the problem. Imagine that you are meeting someone for the first time and walk right up to her with your face an inch from her face. What reaction do you think she has? She would be uncomfortable and move away, or act out with aggression! It is like that in the dog world. Your dog needs to learn the proper way to approach other dogs. If your dog approaches badly, you can encourage the proper approach through training techniques.

Dogs normally do not stare directly into each other's eyes, either. Some breeds have a tendency to do this, though, and can invite aggression.

Encourage nonthreatening behavior in your dog. Your dog should learn to approach other dogs slowly and look away, which tells other dogs he is not a threat. One way to do this is to have him turn his back to an oncoming dog, or drop treats on the ground, which will encourage your dog to look away.

Teach your dog to calm down in stressful situations. If you are out on a walk and your dog is approaching something that is his trigger and may lead to aggression, teach him to follow you and turn away from the object. Have a treat ready and put it near your dog's nose. When he begins to follow the treat, turn so that you are facing away from the object you want to avoid. Use your let's go command at the same time. Give your dog the treat lure after he has completed the turn. Here, you are getting your dog to avoid the object by following you and turning himself in the opposite direction. Then you can continue walking in the opposite direction, or you can put your dog in a down-stay with the threat behind him so he is not focused on it. Continue this for several minutes until your dog's body begins to relax. This also teaches your dog he can learn control in stressful situations.

Where Is It?

The where is it? command essentially trains your dog to look away from the object that may lead to aggression.

1. Drop a treat on the ground and ask your dog, "Where is it?"
2. After he eats the treat and comes back over to you, give him another treat. The goal is to have your dog looking down for the treat and then focusing on you rather than on the distraction you are trying to avoid.
3. Repeat until your dog is quickly running back to you. Make sure you offer the treat every time he comes back to you.
4. Now add the command "let's go" to encourage your dog to walk with you away from the distraction. Be sure to give a treat when the command is done correctly.
5. Keep this up so that your dog is focused either on the treat or you, and then walking with you on-leash.

> ## A DOG WHO BITES
>
> Many forms of aggression can be neutralized with good obedience and a dog learning his proper role in the family and in the world. But if your dog has ever bitten anyone, or if you or others fear your dog, it may be time to seek a specialist's help. Always practice extreme caution with a dog showing signs of aggression.

6. Keep the leash *loose*.
7. Practice this command a lot before you will actually need it in a real-life situation.

7

SPECIAL SITUATIONS

The difference between impossible and the possible
lies in a person's determination.
~Tommy Lasorda~

These additional subjects don't apply to all dogs, but if any do, you'll need to know what to do.

Out of Control at Dog Parks

One of the most important things to do if your dog gets too out of control in the dog park is to exercise him *before* entering. Dog parks are not places where these types of dogs should go to get exercise. Dog parks are for socializing. If your dog enters a dog park in an overly excited state of mind, filled with pent-up energy, problems arise. One of the biggest reasons dogs develop behavior problems is that they are not getting their energy drained enough daily. Most dogs need a lot more exercise than they are getting, and overly excited dogs need even more.

Second, I suggest practicing obedience with your dog daily. Obedience teaches your dog control and helps calm him through that control. If your dog understands a good recall, you will have a lot more control over him while off-leash in the dog park. If your dog is getting too wound up, you can call him over to you and ask for a down-stay until he has relaxed. Or if another dog is displaying behavior that could lead to a negative encounter, you can call your dog over to you and prevent it. Obedience training and lots of exercise are the keys to your dog doing well at the dog park.

Dogs and Cats

Dogs come when they are called;
cats take a message and get back to you.
~Mary Bly~

Teaching dogs and cats to live together harmoniously *is* possible. Some dogs' natural predator drive kicks in when they see something move quickly, like a cat running. It is important to take your dog's focus off the cat immediately and gain control over him with obedience practice. Distract your dog and then reward him for performing an obedience command. This prevents him from reaching the point where he wants to chase. If you can get your dog to perform a down-stay near a cat, that teaches him control before the situation escalates. Brush up on your obedience skills with your dog and practice first at a distance from the cat to work on desensitizing him (see page 164). Slowly work up to maintain the control near the cat. If you practice this well, over time your dog will understand how he is expected to behave near cats.

If you have more than one dog, practice obedience with one dog at a time with leash and collar: sit, down, stay, etc., near the cat. The idea is that your dog learns calm control while being near the cat. You are providing "memory control" for your dog as to what your expectations are. If you have practiced good obedience near the cat for a couple of weeks while on-leash, then one day when your dog is off-leash, he will have that memory of you being the leader and teaching him control. Your guidance will have more effect on him in the moment he needs it.

The key is to prevent your dog from chasing. Observe closely, and if your dog is staring at the cat and not taking his eyes off of her, it is time to do more obedience to redirect that focus. He is allowed to look at the cat, but should then look away and not fixate on her. Chase is preceded by fixation. If you don't allow the fixation, you prevent the attack. Plus, the obedience will help your word have meaning when you ask your dog to change his focus.

If your dog starts to fixate, call him to you and ask for a down-stay with his back to the cat until he relaxes and is no longer fixated. You may have to do this over and over, but if you are consistent and have good timing, your dog will get the message that you as the leader are not going to allow it anymore. When you practice this obedience near the cat, your dog becomes more relaxed around her and will not be sending threatening signals. Your cat will relax more, which further calms your dog.

You decide what is acceptable. Make it very clear to your dog from right now that chasing won't be allowed anymore. This is why I suggest using a leash initially to have good timing and consistency. If you allow your dog to get away with fixation and then the chase 1 time out of 10, you ruin all 9 other times you practiced hard. Be very consistent and practice daily, and soon this problem will be a thing of the past. You will have a harmonious life with all your sweet furry friends. Your cat will thank you too!

Multiple Dogs

If you are considering getting another dog, make sure everyone in the family is ready for it. You will be adding work and expense, so be prepared before making the decision. Ask yourself the following questions:

- Do you have the time to put into training another dog?
- Do you have the money?
- Does your current dog get along with other dogs? Do you have time to make the right match for your family and your current dog?
- Do you have enough space for another dog? Additionally, do you have space to separate them if needed?
- Is your current dog well behaved? Does he consistently respond to your commands?

It is possible that your new dog (let's call her Marge) has the (as yet unidentified) perfect-dog-always-well-behaved gene, but don't count on it. You need to be sure that your current dog (we'll call him Homer) is consistently well behaved at home, on walks, with other dogs, etc., and that he responds to come, sit, down, and all the other commands. Even if Homer is always the perfect gentleman, it is still a good idea to give him a brief refresher course to reinforce his learning. You'll have better results if Marge enters a peaceful and dog-friendly household.

Does Homer have a nearby best friend? It might be a good idea to arrange for a dog sleepover at your house to see how Homer responds to a constant companion. If you notice problems, you can work on them before Marge's arrival. Marge needs to be trained individually. Since my training advice starts out with teaching a dog with no distractions, you need to put Homer in another area. Spend several minutes, several times a day, practicing obedience with Marge. Working with her individually will also communicate that you are in charge.

Later, when Marge is doing well with the commands, practice together with Homer.

Introducing Your New Dog to Your Current Dog

If possible, introduce Marge and Homer before you commit to having them live together. That way, you can change your mind if it doesn't seem like the right match. If you plan to bring Marge home to meet Homer, here are the steps to follow.

1. Get a partner to help.
2. Exercise both dogs separately, if you can, before their meeting.
3. Have them meet in a neutral area away from the home, like a park.
4. You and your partner take the dogs on a walk together, walking in the same direction but not right next to each other. You don't want them to greet face-to-face; getting a smell for each other but not meeting yet. Or, if you prefer, they can meet and smell each other through a fence, like at a tennis court or a base-ball field.
5. When they are ready for the first real meeting, have them meet off-leash first in a fenced-in area. You want to allow a natural greeting, and sometimes leashes prevent that. Or, if you have to use leashes, make sure they are *very* loose. You don't want the tight collar to signal tension.
6. If they play together, that's great! If you notice tension, call each dog away and break the focus a bit. Your goal is to try to make this first meeting a good one.
7. Be calm and relaxed. Take a deep breath in through your nose, slowly exhale through your mouth. You don't want the dogs to pick up on your tension.
8. When you bring Marge to your home for the first time, let her and Homer meet outside first: Then bring Marge inside while your partner stays outside with Homer and plays with him. Marge needs a chance to sniff around on her own a bit first.
9. Don't leave the dogs alone together right away. First watch how they interact.

Don't show favoritism toward either dog. The last thing you want is sibling rivalry. Make sure Marge has her own food and water bowls, bed, and toys. Later Homer and Marge may decide to share, but that is their choice.

DOGFIGHTS

Dogfights can be very dangerous and you should be extremely careful to avoid getting bitten. Never grab a dog's collar to stop a fight. Sometimes spraying dogs with a water hose can break up a fight.

If water isn't available—or the fight is indoors—and you have someone to assist you, each one of you should calmly grab one dog's back legs and pick him or her up (like a wheelbarrow) and begin to walk in a circle away from each other. The dogs have to move their front paws away from each other in order to prevent falling on their faces.

Then immediately separate the dogs into different areas and go cool off yourself. Or, if you are able to, put them both in down-stays away from each other, which gives them and you a chance to calm down.

Do not scream or yell, which can cause even more aggression.

If one dog is too rough or mounts the other over and over, step in once in a while and give the dogs a time-out. If they get too rambunctious, again separate them in different areas, giving each a nice chew bone. You are the leader so you decide what may be needed.

Sometimes step in as a form of prevention too. If the dogs start to show any aggression or threat toward each other, you need to stop the behavior.

TIPS AND WARNINGS
1. Be calm.
2. Separate the dogs immediately—but only if you have help.
3. Do not scream or yell during a dogfight.
4. Never grab a dog by the collar during a dogfight.

Feeding

Should you feed Marge and Homer together or separately? The answer is up to you. If there is so much chaos during mealtime that it is hard for you to control them, then feed them separately, in different rooms if needed. If your dogs do well eating together, that's great. Do what feels right.

Together or separately, put the dogs into a nice calm sit and then put the food bowls in front of them. This rewards your dogs for being calm for mealtime. If you practice this every day consistently, soon your dogs will sit quietly on their own, wait for their food, rather than jumping up and barking or doing some other kind of rowdy behavior. If you put the food down when the dogs are barking or jumping on you, then you reward that behavior and they will do it again next time. If you put the food down only when they are sitting quietly, you reward that behavior and next time they'll sit quietly and wait.

FEEDING TIPS

1. Hold the bowl in front of them and ask them to sit.
2. When they sit, put the food down.
3. Begin increasing the amount of time that you have them wait for their food.
4. Don't allow them to dive into the food, knocking you over. You can control this by putting the food down and having them wait until you give a command to eat.
5. Be clear of your expectations and practice every day.

Some dogs finish quickly and then try to eat the other dog's food. One way to prevent this is to lure that dog away with a nice treat into another area. Or you can teach them to stay near their bowl until you release them.

None of this would be possible if your dogs didn't recognize you as the leader. Having more than one dog is great if you are fully prepared and extremely difficult if you are not. Establish your role as the leader to clearly communicate your expectations.

Senior Dogs

Senior dogs make wonderful companions. They have the wisdom of years behind them and have generally figured out the human world. With the proper care, many dogs live to 14 or 15—that's about 70 to 90 in human years. Smaller dogs tend to live longer than larger breeds. Smaller dogs less than 20 pounds may show their age around 12, but a larger dog may show signs of aging closer to age 8. You may notice a few gradual changes, including graying around the muzzle, he sleeps a little more, or he tires a little easier.

Here is an interesting chart I found on the Senior Dogs Project Web site that shows a dog's age in human years. The dog's weight (size) is an indicator here. According to Dr. Fred L. Metzger, who created this chart, "Senior is the older 'healthy' dog whereas geriatric implies there is some existing health problem like arthritis."

A Dog's Age in Human Years			
Age	Up to 20 lbs	21-50 lbs	51-90 lbs	Over 90 lbs
5	36	37	40	_42_
6	40	42	_45_	_49_
7	_44_	_47_	_50_	_56_
8	_48_	_51_	_55_	_64_
9	_52_	_56_	_61_	_71_
10	_56_	_60_	66	**78**
11	_60_	_65_	72	**86**
12	_64_	69	77	**93**
13	_68_	74	82	**101**
14	72	78	88	**108**
15	76	83	93	**115**
16	80	87	99	**123**
17	84	92	104	Underlined Numbers = Senior
18	88	96	109	
19	92	**101**	115	**_Bold, Italic Numbers =_**
20	96	**105**	120	**_Geriatric_**

Chart developed & permission granted by Dr. Fred L. Metzger, DVM, State College, PA. Courtesy of Pfizer Animal Health.

★ Senior Dog Q & A ★

Q *My trouble is with my 10-year-old dachshund, Earl. I adopted him from a shelter last year. Besides Earl I have a 13-year-old female and 2 older male foster dogs. They are all dachshunds and everybody is spayed/neutered. Earl is a friendly guy, but he usually prefers to keep to himself. In the past 3 weeks or so, Earl has started barking and running toward the foster dogs when they walk past him. They can be 10 feet away and just walking through the room or standing there and he will jump up and run barking at them. The foster boys just keep on walking past or go the other way. Earl never does it to the old lady of the house or my prior male foster who was with us for 5 months, but he did do it with a female foster who went to her new home last week and an annoying young child who visited. I figure he is just protecting his space, but it seems to be getting worse and I'm not sure how to get him to relax and realize there is enough room for everybody.*

A When dogs grow older, their behavior and reactions can change due to physical changes you might not be aware of. It is a good idea to discuss this with your veterinarian and see if there is anything going on physically so that you can work on treatment options to help make Earl more comfortable.

In the meantime, watch for signs of stress and carefully monitor interactions with visitors and among the dogs. There may be times when Earl feels safer and happier hanging out in a quiet place by himself.

In groups of dogs, there is a pack structure where one dog is dominant. Often it is the dog who was there first, usually the older dog. But as the dog ages, or new, younger dogs come into the picture, there can be dominance challenges. You as the guardian have to become the dominant one and use strict control of who gets what and when, while also working on obedience with commands such as sit and down-stay. Close supervision of the dogs may be necessary along with separation when you are not able to watch them.

I also suggest that you put a Gentle Leader head collar on Earl during interactions with visitors. This collar gives you more control over Earl's behavior and it is also believed to help dogs feel calmer because certain pressure points are activated during use. Monitor him and watch for increased signs of stress and stay in contact with your veterinarian. Be cautious, and if you feel Earl could bite someone, you will need to take actions to prevent that.

Q *We have a 15-year-old Lab–Aussie shepherd mix. Venus is still supersharp mentally, but she has very bad hip problems When younger she was always very active, but because of her physical condition it is hard, if not impossible, to keep her stimulated. Most days she gets 2 walks, 20 minutes or so each; she can't walk much longer than that without resting. She can't play ball in the house anymore, which she used to do incessantly. Now she has taken to barking, we suspect just out of boredom. She never barks when we are away, just at us. But as I said, she can't really play anymore, she just hangs out and woofs. Any ideas how we can get Venus to calm down?*

A I understand a little bit about what you are going through because Fax is now in his senior years and experiencing hip problems. Life has begun to change for us as well.

As dogs age, they can undergo physical changes that can affect them in different ways and even alter their behavior. They may vocalize more and show signs of not wanting to be left alone. Painful underlying medical conditions such as arthritis or dental problems are common. A change in vision or hearing can cause sensory problems that also result in changes in behavior. Sometimes even decreased mobility can affect how a dog reacts to events. Discuss this with your veterinarian and see if there are treatment options to help make Venus more comfortable. Be sure to ask what exercise routine may be right for your dog.

I know how important being busy and exercise are for a dog's state of mind, and how difficult it can be on them once these become harder to do because of arthritis. Swimming is great for dogs with arthritis. Water supports joints while providing exercise and stimulation. Look into canine hydrotherapy, which is the use of water to soothe pain and treat some conditions. It can be excellent for aging dogs.

Does Venus like car rides? Fax loves going in the car, so that might be another possibility for providing new sights and smells. Also, try to take her to new places. The sights and smells of a new park while you have a picnic can be quite stimulating and reduce boredom. Just like people, dogs like to explore the world.

Also, talk with your veterinarian about special types of dog massage. Massage can improve circulation and possibly reduce Venus's pain levels. You can do this yourself at home. It will put Venus into a calm state, which may also reduce the barking. Most dogs love massage, and it's a sweet way for you to be together.

Aging in the human and the dog world can be a complex and sometimes difficult time in the lives of the caretakers. Venus may also sense a change in you if you are feeling sorry for her, guilty in some way, or frustrated, and this may make her feel uneasy. Try to maintain the positive attitude that you have always shared with her, maintain clear rules through positive reinforcement, and learn to adapt to changes. Work closely with your veterinarian to be sure everything is being taken care of physically and seek emotional guidance if you feel you need it as well. It is very difficult to watch our beloved pets age, and sometimes we need a little support from family and friends to help us through it.

Training a Deaf Dog

Deaf dogs make great pets. They adapt to their hearing loss quite well because a dog's primary source of communication is through body language and scent. You've probably noticed that when dogs greet each other, they communicate all kinds of signals to each other without any sound but a lot of sniffing.

While barking and growling are additional ways dogs send messages, these aren't their primary methods. In training, too, verbal language isn't necessary. In fact, dogs pay more attention to cues in your body language and facial expressions than to what you are saying to them.

When training any dog, the most important factors are being clear in what you are asking of your dog and rewarding him for the correct behavior. This is true for deaf dogs too. But since they rely on visual cues as opposed to your voice, it's important that you be very precise and clear with your hand signals.

Even though your dog is deaf, it's important that you have the same behavioral expectations you would of any dog. Don't allow your dog to get away with negative behaviors just because you feel sorry for him. He isn't feeling sorry for himself. A well-trained dog is much happier because he gets to spend more time with you and the family. And like all dogs, a deaf dog thrives in a home in which expectations are consistent.

Diabetic Dogs

Just as in people, an increasing number of dogs have diabetes today. Proper exercise and nutrition play an important role in preventing and also coping with this disease. Diabetes is not curable, but the good news is that it is not a death sentence for your dog. Through proper treatment and care your dog could go on to live a normal, full life.

First of all, make sure you completely understand your dog's particular health evaluation from your veterinarian. Write down a list of questions for your vet and get the answers you need. It is important to follow your veterinarian's treatment plan in order to help your dog have the best life possible. If diabetes is not managed well, a lot of serious medical complications can arise.

Proper nutrition and exercise are very important for all dogs, but especially diabetic dogs. Ask your veterinarian what is your dog's ideal weight and help your dog reach that goal. Keep your dog on a regular feeding schedule, offering small meals 2 or 3 times a day at the same time each day to help stabilize blood sugar levels. It is very important for your dog to have a regular exercise schedule as well. Too little or too much exercise at any time can affect your dog's blood sugar levels, so stay on a daily, moderate exercise schedule. Ask your vet how much exercise he or she recommends for your dog. It will take a little extra effort on your part, but once you develop the proper routine, life will become more enjoyable for both you and your dog.

If your dog requires insulin shots, associate the shots with something positive so that your dog does not become fearful. Distract your dog with a very yummy treat while giving the shot. Get the insulin ready to administer and have your dog's favorite treat ready. Offer a treat, give the shot, then offer another treat.

Even though your dog has diabetes, it is important to continue your normal behavioral expectations. Don't allow negative behavior in your dog because you feel sorry for him. A well-trained dog is happier because he gets to spend more time with you and the family, so do not end your training because your dog has diabetes. As with all dogs, yours is happier in a home that has consistent expectations of him.

Your dog's medical needs could change over time, so be sure to have regular checkups with your veterinarian. There are a lot of other people going through the same thing you are, so reaching out to others with diabetic dogs could be beneficial emotionally. Do an

Internet search for "dogs diabetes" and you'll find tons of info sites and chat rooms where you can talk to people in your situation. Enjoy the love your companion dog has to offer you.

Injured Dog Going Stir Crazy

★ Injured Dog Q & A ★

Q Archie is a 3½-year-old neutered male boerboel (South African mastiff). He weighs about 140 pounds. He is fairly well trained and is a very athletic and hyper boy.

The problem is that Archie has injured his right front shoulder and needs to stay calm for a week or so in order to heal. Normally he plays or trains for an hour or more every weekday and more on the weekends. Right now he is stir crazy and is inventing new ways to entertain himself by jumping, running, chewing, and so on. He actually jumped over my dining room table in his excitement. He's also taken to harassing my other dog (12-year-old female) and chasing the cat.

What can I do to help him expend energy without injuring himself? I've tried KONGS, but he is very clever at getting the treats out (even frozen) and then turning the KONG into a self-tossed fetch toy. Because he is a very strong and powerful chewer, chew toys (even Black KONGS) have a very limited lifespan around him. Toys as entertainment don't seem like the best way to go.

I was thinking about teaching Archie a few tricks, but I don't know how or if this is a good idea.

A The very first thing you should do is talk with your veterinarian specifically about what you are going through with Archie. It sounds to me that he might injure himself more by being at home "doing nothing" since he has already jumped over the table! You might also look into canine hydrotherapy, which is beneficial in the recovery program for certain injuries and may drain extra energy at the same time.

I know how important being busy and well exercised is for a dog's state of being, especially a young active one. Does Archie like car rides? That's another way to stimulate his senses. You could even speak with an animal physical therapist. He or she is specially trained to know what kind of exercise could be done for specific injuries.

If Archie is really in need of moving and exercise, it is worth looking into all of these options before he injures himself more at home. Even teaching tricks takes physical movements, so you'll have to get your vet's approval of what can and cannot be done before you start.

After you talk with your vet and an animal physical therapist, and look into hydrotherapy you'll have a better idea of how to release Archie's pent-up energy and speed his healing.

8

FUN THINGS TO DO WITH YOUR DOG

If you never did, you should.
These things are fun, and fun is good.
~Dr. Seuss~

There are so many fun things to do with dogs. The more time you spend with your dog the better, so go out and have fun together. You'll meet a lot of interesting, new people along the way who share your interests.

With so many choices, narrow it down by learning about what your specific breed enjoys. Also, speak with your veterinarian about what kind of activities are appropriate for your dog's health and abilities. Read about what's available in your area. You may be surprised by how many people are in local dog-related clubs, sports, and activities. If you want to try something and can't find it in your area, start your own. The possibilities are endless!

Fetch

All dogs should learn fetch, in my opinion, as long as they are healthy enough to perform it. It is an excellent tool to tire them out and drain pent-up energy.

Teaching Fetch

1. Get a ball or toy that your dog seems really interested in and throw it up in the air, catch it, and even bounce it. You want your dog to get interested in this fun object.

2. Now that your dog seems excited about the object, throw it 4 or 5 feet away—not too far yet.

3. If he goes to get it, brings it back, and drops it for you, throw it again using the command "Fetch!" Each time you can throw the ball a little farther. (Some dogs, especially retrievers, could teach you to fetch. For other breeds, read on.)

4. Some dogs will bring the ball back but won't drop it. In this case, you can have either a hidden second ball that is just as enticing, or a treat so you can do a switch. Show your dog what you plan to swap, and when he drops the ball, treat him and throw it again. If things are going well, have your dog fetch the ball twice before offering the treat upon return, then three times, then randomly until he does it without the treat. Some dogs won't need the treat, because the excitement of your throwing the ball for them is enough of a reward.

5. If your dog drops the ball but immediately goes for it when you try to pick it up, teach the go back command (see page 118).

6. Does your dog want to play chase instead of dropping the ball? Don't move toward him; instead, move away, enticing him to come toward you. When your dog drops the ball, pick it up fast and throw it again.

7. If your dog isn't too motivated, use a special fetch toy with treats inside that he gets to play with only for fetch.

8. If your dog is not yet off-leash trained to come, take caution and play fetch only in a fenced-in area.

Fetch is also fun to play in the water, if your dog enjoys swimming. Over time, you'll learn what works for you and your dog, and you'll be on your way to enjoying a fun game with your dog.

Find It

You can teach your dog to use scent to find things you have hidden and make a game out of it.

1. Excite your dog by showing him a favorite toy or treat.
2. Have your dog in a sit-stay while you place the toy or treat a few feet away.
3. Tell your dog to "Find it" and immediately let him go get it.
4. Give lots of praise when he gets it.
5. Repeat, each time placing the object farther away and eventually hidden in another room.
6. You can even hide the object under a towel or in a box to make the game more challenging.
7. Move the game outdoors and hide the object, first while your dog is watching, and later with his eyes covered or looking away.

This is one of Fax's favorite games. It is so fun to watch him sniff out the scent and then find it.

Tracking

According to the American Kennel Club, "A dog's sense of smell is 100,000 times stronger than a human's. It is said that dogs have 2 billion olfactory receptors, versus 40 million in humans." Because dogs can smell things far better than humans, they make excellent trackers. Tracking is kind of an extension of find it.

Many dogs find tracking one of their favorite things to do. Dogs are evaluated on their ability to follow a path that has been laid out for them, using only their nose. To lay out the track, a human walks a path of up to 1,000 yards and drops an item at the end of it. Up to 2 hours pass to "age the track," and then the dog smells out the path and finds the object at the end. Humans leave behind a unique scent that dogs can detect.

If you are interested in tracking, check your local area and visit a tracking test to see how it all works. You might just find that the experience adds a lot of fun to your and your dog's life.

Tricks

Ring Bells to Go Outside

Through consistency and repetition, you can train your dog to ring bells to go outside and do his business.

1. Hang a set of bells near the door that your dog normally goes out. Hang the bells at a level he can reach.
2. Whenever you take your dog outside, use a command such as "Ring the bells," then *you* ring the bells while your dog is looking, praise him, and immediately go outside. Make sure everyone in your family uses the same command. (Do not use food rewards here or your dog will associate ringing the bells with food instead of going outside.)
3. You must do this consistently and ring the bells *every time* you go outside for this to work.
4. After practicing this for several weeks, say, "Ring the bells," then wait to see if your dog does it for you. If your dog does ring the bells, praise him and immediately let him outside. If your dog doesn't ring the bells, then you ring them, praise him, and let him outside.
5. Repeat the conditioning and your dog will start to do it on his own. If you are in another room and you hear your dog ring the bells, quickly go there, praise him, and let him out. Initially, be quick with your response so he knows he has done the right thing.
6. The key to success is consistency.

Shake Hands

Visitors to your home will be very impressed by this welcome.

1. Take your dog's paw in your hand and say "Shake."
2. Shake your dog's paw and say "Good shake!" while you are shaking his paw.

3. Practice several shakes a day and then see if your dog puts his paw in your hand at your command. If he does, praise and shake.
4. If your dog needs more motivation, you can use a treat.
5. When your dog has the hang of it, let him practice shaking other people's hands.

High Five

After your dog understands how to shake hands, you can teach him to give a high five!

1. Start out similarly to the shake. Put your hand out, but as soon as your dog's paw hits your hand, say "High five" and give a treat.
2. Now each time you put your hand out, gradually raise the height, say "High five," and treat when he taps your hand.
3. Keep practicing several times a day until you can raise your hand in the high five position, give the command, and your dog taps your hand.

Wave

This is fun when guests leave your home.

1. Hold a treat in your hand and show your dog but don't let him have it yet. Encourage him to paw at it by putting your fist close to him.
2. As soon as your dog paws at the treat, open your hand and give the treat.
3. Repeat, this time using the command, "Wave." When your dog paws at your hand, open it and give the treat.
4. When your dog seems to understand the trick, keep your hand just out of reach of your dog so when he goes to paw at it, his paw will wave in the air. Give the command "Wave" when he paws in the air, then treat and praise immediately.

5. Slowly move your hand farther and farther away so that eventually you are actually waving to your dog while you give the command "Wave!"
6. When your dog gets really good at this, start to wean off the treats and instead offer your genuine praise as the reward.

Play Dead (or Take a Nap)

It will be fun to impress your friends and family with your dog's new tricks! Here's a note from a client who was so happy her dog learned this trick: *"Julie, You don't know how happy you've made my husband to teach Riley how to perform the play dead command! He was so excited to show it off to his family. Thanks for everything."*

Playing dead is a popular trick. You can use the command, "Bang," or you can say, "Take a nap" if you prefer.

1. Make sure your dog remembers the down command.
2. Give your dog the command to lie down.
3. Hold a treat and move it over his head so that he rolls onto his side to get it. Give the treat when he rolls to one side.
4. Repeat, using the command "Bang" (or "Take a nap") over and over until your dog begins to lie on his side when you give the command.
5. Your dog may be popping up to receive the treat, so start expecting him to lie still for longer periods of time before treating.
6. Now start to expect your dog to lie completely still with his head on the floor. Wait a second or two at first before treating and gradually extend the amount of time you expect him to wait for the treat.
7. Eventually you'll be able to point your finger, say "Bang," or "Take a Nap" and your dog will perform the full command.

As with all tricks, this takes practice and patience; don't expect your dog to learn instantly. It should be fun for both of you, so if it feels frustrating, come back and try at another time.

Agility

Want an activity to do with your dog that is entertaining for you, exceptional for your dog, a perfect way to spend time with friends and family, and in an environment filled with interesting people who share your interests? Agility is your answer! In this fun dog sport, the handler directs her dog, off-leash, in a race through a prepared obstacle course. Dogs and their handlers have a great time. Some people call it a "playground for dogs." It is an excellent way to challenge your dog's mind while

offering a really pleasurable way to exercise. If you have kids, bring them along — it's a fantastic family activity.

Agility includes obstacle courses with weave poles, pause tables, A-frames, various pole jumps, tire jumps, collapsible tunnels, and teeter-totters. If you get involved in agility, you can buy equipment individually, or you can join a local group in your area. Many people buy or even make equipment for their backyard for fun and practice. Training

your dog to use most of the equipment is fairly easy and will not take too much time. Some of the equipment may take a little more practice, depending on the dog, but the practice will be great stimulation for your dog.

Dogs of all breeds, ages, and sizes can enjoy this entertaining sport with their guardians. Dogs are grouped by size, ability, and sometimes age for competition. The spectrum of this sport spans beginners through serious, advanced players. Some people do it just for fun without the competitive aspect, and others, who love competition, take it pretty seriously. Don't feel intimidated by the more advanced players

when you start. Talk with someone in a local group who might be willing to mentor you as you begin; there also are a lot of books, videos, and online information on the subject.

Find a local group in your area, visit with the other dog guardians and see if it would be something you and your dog would enjoy.

Running

Running with a faithful partner is more fun than running alone. Most dogs are excited to join you, and it's a great workout to drain their pent-up energy for the day. Most young, healthy dogs love to run, but there are a few steps you should take before you start.

1. If you and your dog are not regular runners, then both of you should have a checkup to make sure your bones, joints, heart, etc., are up for the exercise.
2. Start off walking regularly and work your way up to running. This strengthens muscles, builds endurance, and hardens your dog's paw pads in preparation.
3. Warm up with a short walk before diving into a fast-paced run. Muscles need time to warm up and cool down, so also take a little walk after your run.
4. Stretch! The best time to stretch is after you have warmed up your muscles a little, so walk, then stretch, then run.
5. Do not run during hot weather—your dog can easily heat up with that hot fur coat! Run in the early morning or cooler evening.
6. Be aware of how hot the surface of the ground is when you are out. Touch the ground. If it feels hot to you, it will feel hot to your dog's bare paws.
7. Make sure to hydrate yourself and your dog with water.
8. Problems to look out for:

   • Paw pads that are worn down. Talk with your veterinarian about using a special ointment/spray that can protect your dog's paws.
   • Overheating. Warning signs include excessive panting, drooling, and elevated body temperature.
   • Injury or joint problems. Dogs younger than 18 months are not fully developed and should not regularly run, nor should older dogs.

Rollerblading

Rollerblading with your dog is also a great exercise. The rules for running with your dog apply to Rollerblading as well because in both situations your dog is running. Here are some additional tips:

1. You should already be a good Rollerblader before you try to do it with your dog.
2. Practice positive obedience training with your dog so you have more control over his behavior during the session. Teach him not to stop on his own.
3. Wear protective gear, such as a helmet, wrist guards, and knee and elbow pads.
4. Do not use a retractable leash. You want to keep your dog closer, so use a standard leash.
5. If you Rollerblade on a path in a park, try to get your dog to run on the grass next to you to make it easier on his joints and feet.
6. Allow your dog to eliminate before and after the session.

Hiking

Hiking off-leash is one of Fax and my favorite things to do together. I love being in nature, so I especially enjoy hiking in the mountains among all the sounds and beauty of the environment. If your dog is not off-leash trained, you can still enjoy a wonderful hike with him on-leash. If you have not been regularly exercising your dog, build up his endurance (and yours) by starting small.

If you want to add some extra social time to the hike, join a hiking group. Bringing your dog with you on a hike is a great icebreaker, if you tend to be a little on the shy side. There are a variety of hiking options, including family hiking groups, hiking for singles, long hikes, short hikes, overnight camping hikes, and even hikes with stroller accessibilities.

If you wear a backpack when hiking—or even if you don't—consider having your dog wear a special dog backpack. You can condition your dog to enjoy the backpack, and he can carry his own supplies! (See "Exercise!" page 80, for more information on backpacks for dogs.) Be sure your dog is healthy enough and check with your veterinarian just to be sure.

Be prepared with necessary supplies for you and your dog. Bring along a first aid kit that includes bandages, veterinary wrap (compression bandage), and a styptic powder with antiseptic to stop any minor bleeding.

If you plan to hike where there might be wildlife, prepare yourself by learning what to do if you come across a wild animal. Do not let your dog chase wild or domestic animals. Usually the larger animal has the right of way on trails, because it is harder for them to step off the trail. So if you pass a horse, for example, it is courtesy for you to step off the trail with your dog in a controlled stay next to you and allow the horse to pass. Dogs can spook horses, so it is a good idea not to get too close.

Also consider other hikers, because some people are afraid of dogs. Keep your dog close to you while passing by other hikers, rather than letting him run up to say hello.

Be cautious in areas with cliffs or large rocks; your dog may not have a concept of heights. When I first started hiking with Fax, one day we came across a stream below a steep edge on our trail. He loves water! He started heading for the cliff, and I am sure that if I hadn't stopped him he would have fallen down that cliff on his quest to get into the water. I'm glad he had learned the off-leash recall. Many avid hikers suggest using a body harness instead of a neck collar for hiking on-leash, so that if your dog slips over an edge you can get him back up and not accidentally hang him.

Check that dogs are permitted and find out if they are allowed off-leash as well. In addition, consider a flea, tick, and insect repellant before hiking. If you plan to be outside in the sun for extended periods of time, you may even need to apply sunblock to his sun-exposed areas, such as nose and ears (ask your vet for recommendations). Carry plenty of water and some snacks. Bring your cell phone, a compass, and other safety items as needed. Also, make sure your dog has identification or is microchipped. For safety reasons, always let someone know where you plan to hike and when you plan to return.

After the hike, check your dog's paw pads, ears, and nose for any thistles, foxtails, or ticks.

Check out some local waterfalls, wildflower fields, and interesting trails. Just yesterday I was hiking and came across a huge field of sheep with their babies. It was wonderful to walk among them and sit quietly observing as they munched on the green grass along the hill. Fax enjoyed the experience too. The sun was shining and nature was at its best. Around the next hill was a mountain covered in yellow flowers that glowed under the sun. I left the hike feeling refreshed, rejuvenated, and happy. Sharing a day of hiking with your dog, friends, and family, surrounded by nature's beauty, is a wonderful way to live.

Camping

Planning a camping trip? Bring your dog! Being outdoors in nature with all the new smells and sounds is a favorite activity for many dogs.

Here are a few things to prepare for before your camping trip.

1. Double-check that your camping spot allows dogs, and learn the rules for dogs.
2. Apply flea and tick prevention medicine.
3. Make a temporary ID tag with the location of your campground in case your dog wanders off.
4. Bring a first aid kit that includes supplies for your dog.
5. Be sure to include your dog's food, water dish, toys, a couple of good leashes, backpack, a sleeping pad if it's cold, and a crate if your dog can get out of the tent at night.

Hike together during the day and hang out next to the campfire at night! Dogs who are off-leash trained are easier to take camping, so that's one more incentive to work on your off-leash recall.

Swimming

Swimming is fantastic exercise for your dog for the same reasons it is for you. Water offers resistance with low impact on joints. The resistance can make a short swim seem like a long walk, but without the strain on the body, so it's an excellent way to drain your dog's energy. It is also one of the best things you can do for a dog with physical limitations from an injury or arthritis.

Many dogs naturally love swimming, but others need a little persuading at first. Introduce water early so that your dog can learn to love it. Find a nice quiet place with shallow water to begin, and walk in the water with your dog, giving treats and making it all positive. Don't force your dog all the way in and *never* throw him in the water.

Once your dog is comfortable in the water, play fetch with a water toy. Your dog will have great fun retrieving the toy in the water.

If you are not confident your dog can swim well, there are specially designed swim vests for dogs. Make sure your dog has easy access to get out of the water; you don't want him to jump in and not be able to get out. Show your dog how to get out of the water.

Dry your dog's ears after swimming to try to prevent ear infections.

Vacationing with Your Dog

Traveling with a dog has gotten easier as thousands of pet-friendly destinations and lodgings sprout up. There are travel guides that specialize in traveling with your dog, offering information on pet-friendly hotels, outdoor cafés, and local attractions that welcome dogs. Some lodging is so pet-friendly that your pooch will find a basket of treats waiting to welcome him.

There are even camps set up exclusively for people with dogs, offering such amenities as agility, doggy massage, hiking, doggy costume parties, outdoor theaters for you and your dog, dog portraits, dog canoe trips, tail-wagging contests, swimming, tracking, dog babysitting, and more.

Whether you want to go on a "dog vacation" or "vacation with your dog," you'll find numerous choices that can meet the needs of everyone. Research online for more information.

Dog Groups

If you would like to meet new people with your dog, join a dog group. Some groups meet regularly with their dogs for walks, hiking, camping, and singles events. The power of the

Internet has opened up a whole new social world for us humans and our dogs. Dogs are excellent icebreakers for the shy, so whether you are looking to make some new friends or find a lifelong partner, your dog can be a great companion to get you started. Check online to find a dog group in your area.

Therapy Dogs

If your dog is friendly and likes to meet new people and be petted, praised, and massaged, then being a therapy dog might be the perfect career for him. Dog-assisted therapy has been proven to improve people's physical, social, emotional, and cognitive functioning.

Close physical contact with a friendly dog can reduce loneliness. Imagine a senior citizen in a nursing home with few or even no visitors. Now envision how exciting it would be to have a dog come visit! Therapy dogs have been shown to make patients more receptive to medical treatment and nourishment, and to reduce depression. When I first adopted Fax, and he had a little training under his belt, I certified him as a therapy dog and we visited nursing homes together. It was quite a sight for the residents to see a huge, hundred-pound dog walk into the facilty. What smiles Fax brought to their faces! It felt great making someone's day a little brighter.

Dog therapy is also used in rehabilitation units, hospices, children's hospitals, schools, and more. Reading programs have been started using dogs as therapy to encourage readers. This can improve literacy because children with low self-esteem find it easier to read to a dog than to another person. It also tends to make the experience less intimidating and even reduces stress levels, all of which enhance the learning process.

Therapy dogs in children's hospitals are a fantastic way to cheer up sick children too, as you can imagine. They can even help with pain management, physical therapy, and speech problems. There are several organizations that help certify dogs for therapy pet work (do an Internet search for "therapy dogs"). All types of breeds are accepted. Your dog will need a little obedience training for this type of work. The rewards are countless.

Search and Rescue

You've probably seen dogs on the news who have been responsible for a rescue. Your dog can do that too! Many search-and-rescue teams are regular people who volunteer with their dogs. Search and rescue's goal is to save the lives of missing people by responding as quickly as possible, whether for a lost hiker, child, or victim of an avalanche, earthquake, or plane crash.

Because of dogs' extrasensitive hearing and sense of smell, they are extremely valuable in locating missing people. They can reduce search time, which increases the chance that the human can be found alive.

Search-and-rescue dogs are trained to "smell out" the missing human. Humans have a distinct smell that dogs can detect. Using smell, dogs can locate people they cannot actually see.

Here are some examples of search-and-rescue certifications: trailing, land or water search for human remains, avalanche search, and first responder disaster (such as earthquake ruins). Generally, to be involved with search and rescue you need to be physically capable, willing to train, and dedicated to the mission.

Training involves the human learning skills like land navigation, wilderness survival, and first aid. Dogs need to be trainable, have endurance and agility, and get along with other dogs and people. You can get details from the National Association for Search & Rescue (nasar.org) and the American Rescue Dog Association (ardainc.org).

If you are interested in search and rescue but not sure if you could commit to the real-life rescue missions, there are groups that train for fun.

Earthdog Trials

If you have a small terrier, dachshund, or small short-legged mixed breed who likes to bark and dig, check out an Earthdog trial. These dogs were especially bred to hunt rodents underground. Man-made underground tunnels are created with a rat "scent" that the dog must "work" (bark, scratch, dig, etc.). The circumstances are controlled so that neither the dog nor the rat is injured. (If you don't want to use a real rat, go to a pet store for the mate-

rial their rats have urinated on.) Depending on the dog's experience, tunnels can have false exits or entrances, dead ends, several 90-degree turns, and various distractions. Dogs love this game! (You can get info at akc.org/events/earthdog/info.cfm or dirt-dog.com.)

Dock Jumping

Canine dock jumping is a really fun sport. Dogs of all shapes and sizes jump off an elevated dock into water to retrieve their favorite toy. They compete for how far they can jump. It is a lot of fun to watch and participate in, and requires little training. As I was going through the incredible collection of dock-jumping photos from MaxDogPhotos.com, my 5-year old son said he wanted to be a dog because it looked like the dogs were having so much fun! If your dog loves water and has a favorite toy he likes to fetch, you are pretty much ready to try out canine dock jumping.

Flyball

Flyball is a 4-dog team relay race. Teams race against each other and winners are determined by the fastest speed with the fewest errors. The first dog jumps over hurdles to get to a spring-loaded machine he has to tap, which tosses out a tennis ball. The dog catches the ball and runs back over the hurdles to get to the starting line again. When the dog

crosses the line, the next dog goes. The height of the hurdles depends on the size of the dogs, but is usually between 8 and 16 inches high.

Flyball is great for all types of dogs and can be done just for fun or competitively for the serious.

Disc Dogs

Does your dog love to catch a Frisbee? Frisbee disc dogs is a fun sport where dogs are judged on distance catching or even choreographed freestyle.

I was watching a competition one day at a local fair and it came down to two dogs, a standard poodle and a Jack Russell terrier. They both had different ways of catching. The Jack Russell would leap into the air with all his might to catch the Frisbee and the poodle would go over to an area and wait to catch it. Guess who won? The poodle! It was fascinating to watch the intelligence of this creature who knew where the Frisbee would land.

In toss and fetch, the handler has 1 minute to make as many throws as she can while increasing the distance. Dogs get points based on the distance of the throw when they catch it, and receive extra points for midair catches.

Freestyle is a choreographed number where dogs are judged on flips, multiple catches, and even vaulting off objects—including their handler.

Canicross/Bikejoring/Skijoring/ Carting/Scootering

There is no such thing as a hyper dog.
There are only exercise-dependent dogs.
~Kim Tinker, competitive skijorer and scooterer~

Because these sports involve your dog physically pulling you, medium to larger healthy dogs who like to pull enjoy them. The photos show people involved in the competitive side of the sport. If you are not interested in competition, lots of people also do these sports as a hobby, just to have fun with their dogs.

Canicross is basically cross-country walking/hiking/ running while attached to your dog, who is in a special harness. Your dog pulls you and is attached to you with a special belt so your hands are free. This is often the first step in teaching other kinds of pulling sports.

In **bikejoring**, your dog pulls you while you are riding a bike.

In **skijoring**, your dog pulls you while you are cross-country skiing.

Dog carting involves dogs pulling a specially made cart. You can ride the cart, or the cart may carry supplies.

Scootering is kind of like dog sledding but without the snow. Dogs wear the same harness as sled dogs do. The scooter is on wheels instead of skis. Larger dogs can pull alone, or a group of smaller dogs can work as a team.

When starting any new physical activity with your dog, check with your own doctor and your dog's veterinarian to be sure you are both approved for the activity. Be sure to study up on proper safety equipment and procedures so you and your dog can enjoy the experience long-term, without harm. Always wear proper safety equipment, including a helmet and any other gear recommended by those who know the sport. Be careful in warm weather; your dog cannot handle the heat as well as you can. Keep yourself and your dog hydrated with water, and start out slowly to build up both your and your dog's endurance. One of the best ways to introduce yourself to a new dog sport or activity is to learn from others who are knowledgeable about it and do it with their own dogs. Most people are very happy to share their experiences and wisdom on the subject.

LET'S SAVE DOGS' LIVES TOGETHER

You must be the change you want to see in the world.
~Gandhi~

Acording to the ASPCA, half of the dogs in shelters are destroyed simply because there is no one to adopt them. The leading cause of death for healthy dogs is euthanasia in animal shelters.

Ninety-six percent of surrendered dogs have had no training. Dogs are 90 percent less likely to be surrendered when their guardians have access to behavioral advice, according to the No Voice Unheard Web site.

Would you like to know a way to save millions of dogs every year? Read on.

The good news: Millions of dogs are being adopted from shelters and rescue groups. There are approximately 75 million already owned dogs in the United States. While most dogs are obtained through acquaintances and family members, about 16 percent (12 million) are adopted from animal shelters and 5 percent (3.75 million) from rescue groups, according to the National Council of Pet Population Study and Policy and Petfinder.com.

The trend to "adopt" homeless dogs from shelters and rescue organizations is the new in thing. Even celebrities like Oprah Winfrey are joining in. She said on her show that she would never again buy a dog but instead would adopt a homeless dog from either a shelter or a rescue group.

The Humane Society estimates that there are between 4,000 and 6,000 shelters in the United States. There are numerous dog breeds, with more than 800 recognized by various kennel clubs worldwide. Most breeds have dedicated rescue groups, and there are also many other rescue groups taking in all breeds.

Of the 8 million dogs who enter the animal shelters annually, less than half are adopted; the rest are euthanized. According to a national study done by NCPPSP, the dogs most at risk of relinquishment (being given up) soil the house, damage things, are overly active, or are reported as fearful due to the guardian's inappropriate and uneducated response to a dog's natural behavior.

According to the study, we might have been able to keep up to 5 million of those relinquished dogs in their homes if their guardians had learned obedience or had help to get them through the problem behaviors. This is a market in need and an enormous opportunity to save millions of dogs' lives.

The Solution: *Imagine Life with a Well-Behaved Dog*

Dogs are at increased risk of relinquishment if they were obtained at no cost or if their purchase cost was less than $100. This suggests to us that the more money you invest in your dog, and the more educated you are about that dog, the less likely you are to give that dog up. Therefore, the purchase of *Imagine Life with a Well-Behaved Dog* as part of an adoption package can actually decrease the chances that dog will be relinquished to a shelter or rescue group.

Behaviors leading to possible relinquishment can be corrected through the lessons in *Imagine Life with a Well-Behaved Dog* and the ability to communicate directly with me for help.

Prevention is the purpose and direction with which we can make a difference. You and I can do it together.

People with newly adopted dogs can get this book as part of their adoption package at shelters and rescue groups. Each person adopting a dog can come home with this book, as well as the option to communicate online with me so that behavior problems can be prevented, thus keeping the dog in his forever home. In addition to preventing dogs from being returned to the shelter, the book is a source of income for underfunded shelters.

If we can start each dog guardian off with the basics to having a well-behaved dog, we can prevent dogs from being given up, thus reducing the number of dogs who are killed annually. This is a solution to saving dogs' lives!

I plan to donate a portion of my earnings from the sale of each copy of this book toward these causes:

- Decrease the number of healthy, adoptable dogs who are killed simply due to lack of space.
- Improve the adoption process of shelter and rescue dogs to decrease the number of dogs relinquished.
- Help senior dogs get adopted and help with their medical expenses and needs. These wonderful dogs deserve to live out the remainder of their lives in a home, not in a kennel. I have a special place in my heart because of my own senior dog. Thinking about what they have been through their whole lives and all the courage and love they've provided, it makes me sad that many of them are not living out their lives with a family.

I was so excited when I recently discovered the Grey Muzzle Organization at grey muzzle.org. This organization was exactly what I had envisioned creating or supporting. It is a fantastic, well-organized group run by volunteers who share my vision of helping senior dogs. Taken from their Web site: "Grey Muzzle funds programs such as hospice care, senior dog adoption, medical screening, and other special programs to help old dogs at animal welfare organizations across the country." This group is run solely on donations and fund-raising, so if you have seniors in your heart like I do, you may want to offer some support.

It is my goal to reduce the staggering number of dogs killed each year and keep more dogs in their forever homes. Every day, wonderful dogs are being dropped off at shelters and often euthanized. Shelters do their best, but there isn't enough room for all the dogs or enough resources. I know we can improve.

I Can't Do It Alone

Never doubt that a small group of thoughtful,
committed citizens can change the world;
indeed, it's the only thing that ever has.
~Margaret Mead~

If you think you are too small to have an impact,
try going to bed with a mosquito.
~Anita Roddick~

If you have been helped by something in this book, or like being able to talk one-on-one through my Web site for support and encouragement, imagine how many others can also be helped. We could potentially save thousands or even millions of dogs' lives by offering solutions to keeping those dogs in their forever homes. To do this, I need your help, and I have some really simple things you can do right now:

- Contact your local animal shelter and breed rescue groups to suggest that they provide *Imagine Life with a well-Behaved Dog* in their new adoption packages. Let them know this could be part of a solution to help improve success rates of adoptions and save dogs' lives and help the people who adopt their dogs.
- Let them know the sale of the book can also offer them a source of much-needed income to help the dogs they care for now through special discounts. Also inform them of the included Web site promotion that offers one-on-one guidance working toward solutions.
- Contact your local bookstores and pet stores and request they put the book on their shelves. Imagine how many people walk into the store, feeling desperate to resolve a behavior problem and close to giving their dog up. Perhaps we can help them keep their dogs.

- If you think the information in this book could help keep some dogs in their forever homes and prevent their euthanasia, you can spread the word by writing positive reviews through sites like Amazon.com, Barnesandnoble.com, and Borders.com. Many people who struggle with their dogs look to these sites to find a book that can help them.

My goal is to help every guardian have a better, happier life with his or her dog and do everything I can to lower the rates of euthanasia by improving adoption support and reducing the number of dogs returned to shelters.

I know that with your help to spread the word, we can really make a difference. If you need further inspiration, walk into a shelter and see the desperate dogs who need homes. Where did they come from? How many dogs have been euthanized at *your* local shelter? Ask. Be informed. Information is power.

If you share my passion and want to know more, contact me at www.webDog Trainer.com. If you have other ideas to help, I'd love to hear them! Bringing together the power of many is what can make a difference. If you were successful at getting the message about the book out there, let me know. If you got your local shelter or rescue groups to put the book in their adoption packages, I want to hear about it. I can write updates through the site to keep you informed of our progress for saving dogs.

> *If not now, when?*
> *~Talmud~*

For those of you already involved in animal rescue, through your efforts in shelters and rescue groups, and as fosterers, I wholeheartedly thank you for your hard work. If you know someone who has made a difference, let me know. I'd love to spotlight people on my Web site as a show of appreciation.

With your help, we can make a difference.

CONCLUSION LETTER FROM JULIE

I hope you've enjoyed the program and that your dog is better behaved than when you started.

Remember, having a well-behaved dog comes from taking the information you've learned from this program and using it in your daily life with your dog. Your consistency, timing, patience, and calm, clear leadership are the determining factors in how well your dog does.

Think of how proud you will be of yourself and your dog, and how proud your dog will be of himself.

Keep up the good work, and remember, training never ends; it just becomes a natural part of your life with your dog.

> *The greatness of a nation and its moral progress*
> *can be judged by the way its animals are treated.*
> *~Gandhi~*

Contact me whenever you need additional guidance. I am here for you.
Now go enjoy life with your dog!
All the best,

Julie

PHOTO CREDITS

All photos courtesy of the author except for the following:

Page 6: istockphoto

Page 8, top: istockphoto

Page 8, bottom: Aerial Gilbert

Page 11: Amber-Dawn M. Conway, Berea ARF

Page 19: istockphoto

Page 20: istockphoto

Page 21: Amber-Dawn M. Conway, Berea ARF

Page 25: Lisa Schermerhorn, K-9 Photography

Page 29: istockphoto

Page 32: sxc.hu

Page 36: Courtesy of KONG Company

Page 37: istockphoto

Page 64: stockexpert.com

Page 69: istockphoto

Page 74: sxc.hu

Page 84: Nate Jolly

Page 94: Nate Jolly

Page 140: Lisa Schermerhorn, K-9 Photography

Page 144: Lisa Schermerhorn, K-9 Photography

Page 145: Lisa Schermerhorn, K-9 Photography

Page 152: Moriya Halon

Page 156: istockphoto

Page 179: istockphoto

Page 181: istockphoto

Page 182: Steve Oppenheimer

Page 194: sxc.hu

Page 197: sxc.hu

Page 199, top: Lisa Schermerhorn, K-9 Photography

Page 199, bottom: Howard George, www.maxdog photos.com

Page 207, top: Lisa Schermerhorn, K-9 Photography

Page 207, bottom: Howard George, www.maxdog photos.com

Page 208, top: Howard George, www.maxdog photos.com

Page 208, bottom left: Howard George, www .maxdogphotos.com

Page 208, bottom right: Lisa Schermerhorn, K-9 Photography

Page 209: Howard George, www.maxdogphotos .com

Page 210: Filip Chludil, www.fchfoto.cz

Page 211: Filip Chludil, www.fchfoto.cz

Page 212: Filip Chludil, www.fchfoto.cz

Page 213: sxc.hu

Page 219: Howard George, www.maxdogphotos .com

INDEX

DO YOU NEED MORE HELP WITH YOUR DOG?

Would you like to talk to me about your dog?

Do you need some help solving a specific problem or just need a little encouragement or motivation?

You can contact me directly by going to my Web site: www.webDogTrainer.com.

Readers of this book receive a special, discounted rate for direct, one-on-one contact with me when using the special promo code: **IMAGINE**

I am here for you,

Julie